Anonymous

Case presented on the part of the government of Her Britannic Majesty

To the Tribunal of Arbitration constituted under article I of the treaty concluded at Washington on the 29th February, 1892

Anonymous

Case presented on the part of the government of Her Britannic Majesty
To the Tribunal of Arbitration constituted under article I of the treaty concluded at
Washington on the 29th February, 1892

ISBN/EAN: 9783337868932

Printed in Europe, USA, Canada, Australia, Japan

Cover: Foto ©ninafisch / pixelio.de

More available books at **www.hansebooks.com**

UNITED STATES. No. 1 (1893).

BEHRING SEA ARBITRATION.

CASE

PRESENTED ON THE PART OF THE

GOVERNMENT OF HER BRITANNIC MAJESTY

TO THE

TRIBUNAL OF ARBITRATION

CONSTITUTED UNDER ARTICLE I OF THE TREATY CONCLUDED AT WASHINGTON ON THE 29TH FEBRUARY, 1892,

BETWEEN

HER BRITANNIC MAJESTY AND THE UNITED STATES OF AMERICA.

Presented to both Houses of Parliament by Command of Her Majesty.
March 1893.

LONDON:
PRINTED FOR HER MAJESTY'S STATIONERY OFFICE
BY HARRISON AND SONS, ST. MARTIN'S LANE,
PRINTERS IN ORDINARY TO HER MAJESTY.

And to be purchased, either directly or through any Bookseller, from
EYRE AND SPOTTISWOODE, EAST HARDING STREET, FLEET STREET, E.C., AND
32, ABINGDON STREET, WESTMINSTER, S.W.; or
JOHN MENZIES & Co., 12, HANOVER STREET, EDINBURGH, AND
90, WEST NILE STREET, GLASGOW; or
HODGES, FIGGIS & Co., Limited, 104, GRAFTON STREET, DUBLIN.

GENERAL CONTENTS.

The Case now submitted to the Arbitrators on the part of the Government of Her Britannic Majesty contains a statement of the facts which that Government considers to be material to enable the Arbitrators to arrive at a just conclusion upon the points submitted to them by the Treaty of Arbitration.

It contains also some general propositions which that Government believes to be in accordance with the established principles of International Law, and upon which it intends to rely.

The Case is arranged as follows:—

		Pages.
	Introductory Statement and Outline of Argument	1–9
	Arrangement of Case and Heads of Argument	9–13
Chapter I, Head (A).	The User, up to the year 1821, of the Waters of Behring Sea and other Waters of the North Pacific	13–36
Chapter II, Head (B).	The Ukase of 1821, and the circumstances connected therewith leading up to the Treaties of 1824 and 1825	37–58
Chapter III, Head (C).	The question whether the body of Water now known as Behring Sea is included in the phrase "Pacific Ocean," as used in the Treaty of 1825 between Great Britain and Russia	59–76
Chapter IV, Head (D).	The User of the Waters in question from 1821 to 1867	77–90
Chapter V, Head (E).	What rights passed to the United States under the Treaty of 30th March, 1867	91–102
Chapter VI, Head (F).	The action of the United States and Russia from 1867 to 1886 ..	103–120
Chapter VII, Head (G).	Various contentions of the United States since the year 1886 ..	121–134
Chapter VIII.	Has the United States any right, and, if so, what right, of protection or property in the Fur-Seals frequenting the Islands of the United States in Behring Sea when such seals are found outside the ordinary 3-mile limit?	135–140
Chapter IX.	General Conclusions upon the whole Case	141–157
Chapter X.	Recapitulation of Argument	158–160
	Conclusion	161

BEHRING SEA ARBITRATION.

Case presented on behalf of the Government of Her Britannic Majesty to the Tribunal of Arbitration.

INTRODUCTORY STATEMENT.

Introductory Statement.

THE differences between Great Britain and the United States of America, the subject of this Arbitration, arise out of claims by the United States of America to prevent and interfere with British vessels fishing in the waters of Behring Sea other than the territorial waters thereof.

Prior to the year 1886 British vessels had, in common with the vessels of the United States and those of other nations, navigated and fished in the non-territorial waters of Behring Sea without interference.

Seizures of British ships.

In 1886 the British schooner "Thornton" was arrested when fishing 70 miles south-east of St. George Island, the nearest land.

The vessel was libelled in the United States' District Court of Alaska by the District Attorney, the charge formulated being that the vessel was "found engaged in killing fur-seals within the limits of Alaska Territory and in the waters thereof, in violation of Section 1056 of the Revised Statutes of the United States."

The vessel was condemned, and the master and mate were imprisoned and fined.

The British schooners "Carolena" and "Onward" were seized about the same time when fishing under similar circumstances, and were subsequently condemned by the District Court.

The Judge (in summing up the case of the "Thornton") ruled that the Law above mentioned applied to all the waters of Behring Sea east of 193° of west longitude.

Certain other vessels were also subsequently seized in non-territorial waters, and the fishing of British vessels was interfered with under the circumstances hereinafter stated.

Great Britain protested against this action on the part of the United States, and negotiations took place, which eventually resulted in the Treaty and Convention entered into at Washington on the 20th February and the 18th April, 1892.

The Treaty is as follows:—

50th Cong., 2nd Sess., Senate Ex. Doc. No. 106, pp. 120–130.
Blue Book, United States, No. 2, 1890, pp. 2, 19, 30.
See Appendix, vol. iii.

"Her Majesty the Queen of the United Kingdom of Great Britain and Ireland and the United States of America, being desirous to provide for an amicable settlement of the questions which have arisen between their respective Governments concerning the jurisdictional rights of the United States in the waters of Behring Sea, and concerning also the preservation of the fur-seal in or habitually resorting to the said sea, and the rights of the citizens and subjects of either country as regards the taking of fur-seal in or habitually resorting to the said waters, have resolved to submit to arbitration the questions involved, and to the end of concluding a Convention for that purpose have appointed as their respective Plenipotentiaries:

"Her Majesty the Queen of the United Kingdom of Great Britain and Ireland, Sir Julian Pauncefote, G.C.M.G., K.C.B., Her Majesty's Envoy Extraordinary and Minister Plenipotentiary to the United States; and the President of the United States of America, James G. Blaine, Secretary of State of the United States;

"Who, after having communicated to each other their respective Full Powers, which were found to be in due and proper form, have agreed to and concluded the following Articles:—

"ARTICLE I.

"The questions which have arisen between the Government of Her Britannic Majesty and the Government of the United States concerning the jurisdictional rights of the United States in the waters of Behring Sea, and concerning also the preservation of the fur-seal in or habitually resorting to the said sea, and the rights of the citizens and subjects of either country as regards the taking of fur-seal in or habitually resorting to the said waters, shall be submitted to a Tribunal of Arbitration, to be composed of seven Arbitrators, who shall be appointed in the following manner, that is to say: two shall be named by Her Britannic Majesty; two shall be named by the President of the United States; his Excellency the President of the French Republic shall be jointly requested by the High Contracting Parties to name one; His Majesty the King of Italy shall be so requested to name one; and His Majesty the King of Sweden and Norway shall be so requested to name one. The seven Arbitrators to be so named shall be jurists of distinguished reputation in their respective countries; and the selecting Powers shall be requested to choose, if possible, jurists who are acquainted with the English language.

"In case of the death, absence, or incapacity to serve of any or either of the said Arbitrators, or in the event of any or either of the said Arbitrators omitting or declining or ceasing to act as such, Her Britannic Majesty, or the President of the United States, or his Excellency the President of the French Republic, or His Majesty the King of Italy, or His Majesty the King of Sweden and Norway, ı the case may be, shall name, or shall be requested to name forthwith, another person to act as Arbitrator in the place and stead of the Arbitrator originally named by such head of a State.

"And in the event of the refusal or omission for two months after receipt of the joint request from the High Contracting Parties of his Excellency the President of the French Republic, or His Majesty the King of Italy, or His Majesty the King of Sweden and Norway, to name an Arbitrator, either to fill the original appointment or to fill a vacancy as above provided, then in such case the appointment shall be made or the vacancy shall be filled in such manner as the High Contracting Parties shall agree.

"ARTICLE II.

"The Arbitrators shall meet at Paris within twenty days after the delivery of the Counter-Cases mentioned in Article IV, and shall proceed impartially and carefully to examine and decide the questions that have been or shall be laid before them as herein provided on the part of the Governments of Her Britannic Majesty and the United States respectively. All questions considered by the Tribunal, including the final decision, shall be determined by a majority of all the Arbitrators.

"Each of the High Contracting Parties shall also name one person to attend the Tribunal as its Agent to represent it generally in all matters connected with the arbitration.

"ARTICLE III.

"The printed Case of each of the two parties, accompanied by the documents, the official correspondence, and other evidence on which each relies, shall be delivered in duplicate to each of the Arbitrators and to the Agent of the other party as soon as may be after the appointment of the members of the Tribunal, but within a period not exceeding four months from the date of the exchange of the ratifications of this Treaty.

"ARTICLE IV.

"Within three months after the delivery on both sides of the printed Case, either party may, in like manner, deliver in duplicate to each of the said Arbitrators, and to the Agent of the other party, a Counter-Case, and additional documents, correspondence, and evidence, in reply to the Case, documents, correspondence, and evidence so presented by the other party.

"If, however, in consequence of the distance of the place from which the evidence to be presented is to be procured, either party shall, within thirty days after the receipt by its Agent of the Case of the other party, give notice to the other party that it requires additional time for the delivery of such Counter-Case, documents, correspondence, and evidence, such additional time so indicated, but not exceeding sixty days beyond the three months in this Article provided, shall be allowed.

"If in the Case submitted to the Arbitrators either party shall have specified or alluded to any Report or document in its own exclusive possession, without annexing a copy, such party shall be bound, if the other party thinks proper to apply for it, to furnish that party with a copy thereof; and either party may call upon the other, through the Arbitrators, to produce the originals or certified copies of any papers adduced as evidence, giving in each instance notice thereof within thirty days after delivery of the Case; and the original or copy so requested shall be delivered as soon as may be, and within a period not exceeding forty days after receipt of notice.

"ARTICLE V.

"It shall be the duty of the Agent of each party, within one month after the expiration of the time limited for the delivery of the Counter-Case on both sides, to deliver in duplicate to each of the said Arbitrators and to the Agent of the other party a printed argument showing the points and referring to the evidence upon which his Government relies, and either party may also support the same before the Arbitrators by oral argument of counsel; and the Arbitrators may, if they desire further elucidation with regard to any point, require a written or printed statement or argument, or oral argument by counsel, upon it; but in such case the other party shall be entitled to reply either orally or in writing, as the case may be.

"ARTICLE VI.

"In deciding the matters submitted to the Arbitrators, it is agreed that the following five points shall be submitted to them, in order that their award shall embrace a distinct decision upon each of said five points, to wit:—

"1. What exclusive jurisdiction in the sea now known as the Behring Sea, and what exclusive rights in the seal fisheries therein, did Russia assert and exercise prior and up to the time of the cession of Alaska to the United States?

Treaty of 1892.

Questions for the decision of the Tribunal.

Treaty of 1892.

"2. How far were these claims of jurisdiction as to the seal fisheries recognised and conceded by Great Britain?

"3. Was the body of water now known as the Behring Sea included in the phrase 'Pacific Ocean,' as used in the Treaty of 1825 between Great Britain and Russia; and what rights, if any, in the Behring Sea, were held and exclusively exercised by Russia after said Treaty?

"4. Did not all the rights of Russia as to jurisdiction, and as to the seal fisheries in Behring Sea east of the water boundary, in the Treaty between the United States and Russia of the 30th March, 1867, pass unimpaired to the United States under that Treaty?

"5. Has the United States any right, and, if so, what right, of protection or property in the fur-seals frequenting the islands of the United States in Behring Sea when such seals are found outside the ordinary 3-mile limit?

"ARTICLE VII.

"If the determination of the foregoing questions as to the exclusive jurisdiction of the United States shall leave the subject in such position that the concurrence of Great Britain is necessary to the establishment of Regulations for the proper protection and preservation of the fur-seal in, or habitually resorting to, the Behring Sea, the Arbitrators shall then determine what concurrent Regulations outside the jurisdictional limits of the respective Governments are necessary, and over what waters such Regulations should extend, and to aid them in that determination, the Report of a Joint Commission, to be appointed by the respective Governments, shall be laid before them with such other evidence as either Government may submit.

"The High Contracting Parties furthermore agree to co-operate in securing the adhesion of other Powers to such Regulations.

"ARTICLE VIII.

"The High Contracting Parties having found themselves unable to agree upon a reference which shall include the question of the liability of each for the injuries alleged to have been sustained by the other, or by its citizens, in connection with the claims presented and urged by it; and, being solicitous that this subordinate question should not interrupt or longer delay the submission and determination of the main questions, do agree that either may submit to the Arbitrators any question of fact involved in said claims, and ask for a finding thereon, the question of the liability of either Government upon the facts found to be the subject of further negotiation.

"ARTICLE IX.

"The High Contracting Parties having agreed to appoint two Commissioners on the part of each Government to make the joint investigation and Report contemplated in the preceding Article VII, and to include the terms of the said Agreement in the present Convention, to the end that the joint and several Reports and recommendations of said Commissioners may be in due form submitted to the Arbitrators, should the contingency therefor arise, the said Agreement is accordingly herein included as follows :—

"Each Government shall appoint two Commissioners to investigate, conjointly with the Commissioners of the other Government, all the facts having relation to seal life in Behring Sea, and the measures necessary for its proper protection and preservation.

"The four Commissioners shall, so far as they may be able to agree, make a joint Report to each of the two Governments, and they shall also report, either jointly or severally, to each Government on any points upon which they may be unable to agree.

"These Reports shall not be made public until they shall be submitted to the Arbitrators, or it shall appear that the contingency of their being used by the Arbitrators cannot arise.

"ARTICLE X.

"Each Government shall pay the expenses of its members of the Joint Commission in the investigation referred to in the preceding Article.

"ARTICLE XI.

"The decision of the Tribunal shall, if possible, be made within three months from the close of the argument on both sides.

"It shall be made in writing and dated, and shall be signed by the Arbitrators who may assent to it.

"The decision shall be in duplicate, one copy whereof shall be delivered to the Agent of Great Britain for his Government, and the other copy shall be delivered to the Agent of the United States for his Government.

"ARTICLE XII.

"Each Government shall pay its own Agent, and provide for the proper remuneration of the counsel employed by it and of the Arbitrators appointed by it, and for the expense of preparing and submitting its case to the Tribunal. All other expenses connected with the Arbitration shall be defrayed by the two Governments in equal moieties.

"ARTICLE XIII.

"The Arbitrators shall keep an accurate record of their proceedings, and may appoint and employ the necessary officers to assist them.

"ARTICLE XIV.

'The High Contracting Parties engage to consider the result of the proceedings of the Tribunal of Arbitration as

Treaty of 1892.

a full, perfect, and final settlement of all the questions referred to the Arbitrators.

"ARTICLE XV.

"The present Treaty shall be duly ratified by Her Britannic Majesty and by the President of the United States of America, by and with the advice and consent of the Senate thereof; and the ratifications shall be exchanged either at Washington or at London within six months from the date hereof, or earlier if possible.

"In faith whereof, we, the respective Plenipotentiaries, have signed this Treaty, and have hereunto affixed our seals.

"Done in duplicate, at Washington, the 29th day of February, 1892.

   (L.S.) "JULIAN PAUNCEFOTE.
   (L.S.) "JAMES G. BLAINE."

Outline of Argument.

Outline of Argument.

The general outline of the argument submitted to the Tribunal of Arbitration on behalf of Great Britain will be as follows:—

That Behring Sea, as to which the question arises, is an open sea in which all nations of the world have the right to navigate and fish, and that the rights of navigation and fishing cannot be taken away or restricted by the mere declaration or claim of any one or more nations; they are natural rights, and exist to their full extent unless specifically modified, controlled, or limited by Treaty.

That no mere non-user or absence of exercise has any effect upon, nor can it in any way impair or limit such rights of nations in the open seas. They are common rights of all mankind.

In support of these principles, which are clearly established, and have never been seriously disputed by jurists, authorities will be cited.

That in accordance with these principles, and in the exercise of these rights, the subjects and vessels of various nations did from the earliest times visit, explore, navigate, and trade in the sea in question, and that the exercise of these natural rights continued without any attempted **interference or control by Russia down to the year 1821.**

Outline of Argument.

That in 1821 when Russia did attempt by Ukase, *i.e.*, by formal declaration, to close to other nations, the waters of a great part of the Pacific Ocean (including Behring Sea) Great Britain and the United States immediately protested against any such attempted interference, maintaining the absolute right of nations to navigate and fish in the non-territorial waters of Behring Sea and other non-territorial waters of the Pacific Ocean. Both countries asserted that these rights were common national rights, and could not be taken away, or limited by Ukase, Proclamation, or Declaration, or otherwise than by Treaty.

That in the years 1824 and 1825, in consequence of these protests, Russia unconditionally withdrew her pretensions, and concluded Treaties with the United States and with Great Britain which recognized the rights common to the subjects of those countries to navigate and fish in the non-territorial waters of the seas over which Russia had attempted to assert such pretentions.

That from the date of such Treaties down to the year 1867 (in which year a portion of the territories which had been referred to in and affected by the Ukase of Russia in the year 1821, was purchased by and ceded to the United States,) the vessels of several nations continued, year by year, in largely increasing numbers, to navigate, trade, and fish in the waters of Behring Sea, and that during the whole of that period of nearly fifty years there is no trace of any attempt on the part of Russia to reassert or claim any dominion or jurisdiction over the non-territorial waters of that sea, but, on the contrary, the title of all nations to navigate, fish, and exercise all common rights therein was fully recognized.

That on the purchase and acquisition of Alaska by the United States in the year 1867, the United States were fully aware and recognized that the rights of other nations to navigate and fish in the non-territorial waters adjacent to their newly-acquired territory, existed in their full natural state, unimpaired and unlimited by any Treaty or bargain whatever.

That, from the year 1867 down to the year 1886, the United States, while they lawfully and properly controlled and legislated for the shores and territorial waters of their newly-acquired

Outline of Argument.	territory, did not attempt to restrict or interfere with the rights of other nations to navigate and fish in the non-territorial waters of Behring Sea or other parts of the Pacific Ocean.

That, under changed conditions of territorial ownership, and in view of certain new circumstances which had arisen in consequence of the growth of the industry of pelagic sealing in non-territorial waters, the United States reverted, in the first instance, to certain claims based upon those of the Russian Ukase of 1821, which the United States, together with Great Britain, had successfully contested at the time of their promulgation; but in the course of the discussions which have arisen, these exceptional claims to the control of non-territorial waters were dropped, and in their place various unprecedented and indefinite claims put forward, which appear to be based upon an alleged property in fur-seals as such.

Finally, that while Great Britain has from the first strenuously and consistently opposed all the foregoing exceptional pretensions and claims, she has throughout been favourably disposed to the adoption of general measures of control of the fur-seal fishery, should these be found to be necessary or desirable with a view to the protection of the fur-seals, provided that such measures be equitable and framed on just grounds of common interest, and that the adhesion of other Powers be secured, as a guarantee of their continued and impartial execution.

Arrangement of Case.

Arrangement of Case.	It will be convenient to state the arrangement and order of the Case here presented on behalf of Great Britain.
Article VI.	The first three points of Article VI are as follows:—

"1. What exclusive jurisdiction in the sea now known as the Behring Sea, and what exclusive rights in the seal fisheries therein, did Russia assert and exercise prior and up to the time of the cession of Alaska to the United States?

"2. How far were these claims of jurisdiction as to the seal fisheries recognized and conceded by Great Britain?

"3. Was the body of water now known as the Behring Sea included in the phrase 'Pacific Ocean,' as used in the Treaty of 1825 between Great Britain and Russia; and what rights, if any, in the Behring Sea, were held and exclusively exercised by Russia after the said Treaty?"

Arrangement of Case.

It is proposed in the first instance to deal with these points, which relate to the original claims by Russia to certain rights in Behring Sea, and the action of Great Britain respecting these claims.

The questions therein raised will be considered under the following heads:—

Heads of Argument.

(A.) The user up to the year 1821 of Behring Sea and other waters of the North Pacific. — Chapter I. Head A.

(B.) The Ukase of 1821 and the circumstances connected therewith leading up to the Treaties of 1824 and 1825. — Chapter II. Head B.

(C.) The question whether the body of water now known as Behring Sea is included in the phrase "Pacific Ocean," as used in the Treaty of 1825 between Great Britain and Russia. — Chapter III. Head C.

(D.) The user of the waters in question from 1821 to 1867. — Chapter IV. Head D.

It is then proposed to consider point 4 of Article VI, which is as follows:—

"4. Did not all the rights of Russia as to jurisdiction and as to the seal fisheries in Behring Sea east of the water boundary, in the Treaty between the United States and Russia of the 30th March, 1867, pass unimpaired to the United States under that Treaty?"

This point will be considered under the following heads:—

(E.) What rights passed to the United States under the Treaty of Cession of March 30, 1867. — Chapter V. Head E.

(F.) The action of the United States and Russia from 1867 to 1886. — Chapter VI. Head F.

(G.) The various contentions advanced by the United States since the year 1886. — Chapter VII. Head G.

Point 5 of Article VI is as follows:—

"Has the United States any right, and, if so, what right, of protection or property in the fur-seals frequenting — Chapter VIII. Article VI, Point 5

11

Arrangement of Case.

the islands of the United States in Behring Sea when such seals are found outside the ordinary 3-mile limit?"

This will be briefly considered, but the proposition which appears to be embodied in this question is of a character so unprecedented that, in view of the absence of any precise definition, it is impossible to discuss it at length at the present time. It will, however, be treated in the light of such official statements as have hitherto been made on the part of the United States, its discussion in detail being necessarily reserved till such time as the United States may produce the evidence or allegations upon which it relies in advancing such a claim.

Article VII is as follows:—

Article VII.

"If the determination of the foregoing questions as to the exclusive jurisdiction of the United States shall leave the subject in such position that the concurrence of Great Britain is necessary to the establishment of Regulations for the proper protection and preservation of the fur-seal in, or habitually resorting to, the Behring Sea, the Arbitrators shall then determine what concurrent Regulations outside the jurisdictional limits of the respective Governments are necessary, and over what waters such Regulations should extend, and to aid them in that determination, the Report of a Joint Commission, to be appointed by the respective Governments, shall be laid before them, with such other evidence as either Government may submit.

"The High Contracting Parties furthermore agree to co-operate in securing the adhesion of other Powers to such Regulations."

The terms of this Article make it necessary that the consideration of any proposed Regulations should be postponed until the decision of the Tribunal has been given on the previous questions.

Beyond, therefore, demonstrating that the concurrence of Great Britain is necessary to the establishment of any Regulations which have for their object the limitation or control of the rights of British subjects in regard to seal fishing in non-territorial waters, it is not proposed to discuss the question of the proposed Regulations, or the nature of the evidence which will be submitted to the Tribunal.

Article VIII.

With regard to the points raised under Article VIII (which refer to questions arising out of claims for damages), it will be contended on behalf of Great Britain that the seizure of the ships was unlawful, and the Arbitrators will be asked to find that in each case the seizure took place in non-territorial waters, that such seizures were made with the authority and on behalf of the Government of the United States, and that the amounts of damages with Great Britain is entitled to claim on behalf of the owners, masters, and crews are the respective amounts stated in the Schedule of particulars appended to this Case.

Arrangement of Case.

CHAPTER I.

User of Waters up to 1821.

HEAD (A).—*The User, up to the year 1821, of the Waters of Behring Sea and other Waters of the North Pacific.*

It is shown in the following series of historical notes, chronologically arranged, that the waters subsequently included in the claim made by Russia under the Ukase of 1821, had been freely navigated over, and frequented for purposes of trade and for other purposes, by ships of various nations, from the earliest times. Further, that the discovery and exploration of these waters and the coasts and islands washed by them, was largely due to the navigators of various nations, and in particular to those of Great Britain.

Area to be considered.

The waters affected by the Russian Ukases of 1799 and 1821[*] include not only the entire area of Behring Sea (though that sea is not specifically mentioned by any name in either Ukase), but also other parts of the Pacific Ocean, and in considering the nature of the user of the waters now in question, the entire area affected by the Ukase of 1821 is included, the facts relating to all parts of this area being of equal significance.

It will be noted in this connection that the limit claimed under the Ukase extended southward to the 51st parallel of north latitude on the American coast; and that, therefore, any events occurring to the north of 54° 40′, which is the southernmost point of the territory now known as Alaska, are well within this limit.

" Pacific Ocean "

The Pacific Ocean as a whole, was, in the last century and in the early part of the present century, variously named the *Pacific*, or *Great Ocean* or *South Sea*, the last name arising from the circumstance that it had been reached by sailing southward round the Cape of Good Hope or Cape Horn.

" Behring Sea."

Behring Sea is, and was at the time of the negotiations which arose immediately on the promulgation of the Ukase of 1821, recognized by geographers as a part of the Pacific Ocean.

---

[*] The text of the Ukase of 1799 will be found at p. 25 of this Case; that of the Ukase of 1821 at . 37.

The name by which it is now known is that of the navigator Behring, but in earlier times it was often named the Sea of Kamtchatka.

Description of Behring Sea.

This sea washes the northern parts of the coasts of North America and of Asia, and is regarded as extending from Behring Strait on the north to the Aleutian and Commander Islands on the south. Its area is at least two-thirds of that of the Mediterranean, and more than twice that of the North Sea, while its extreme width is 1,200 miles. From north to south it extends over about 14 degrees of latitude, or more than 800 miles.

From the south it is approached by numerous open sea-ways, one of which is 175 miles wide, another 95 miles, five more from 55 to 22 miles, and very many of smaller width.

On the north, it communicates with the Arctic Ocean by Behring Strait, 48 miles in width.

Behring Sea is the common highway to the Arctic Ocean with its valuable fisheries. It is Great Britain's highway to her possessions in the north viâ the Yukon River (of which the free navigation is guaranteed by Treaty), as well as the route for such communication as may be held or attempted with the northern parts of the coasts of North America to the east of Alaska, and with the estuary of the great Mackenzie River.

Treaty of Washington, May 8, 1871, Article XXVI.

Historical Outline.

In 1728 and 1729, Behring, in his first expedition, outlined, somewhat vaguely, the Asiatic coast of Behring Sea, and practically proved the separation of the Asiatic and American continents.

Historical Outline

Bancroft, History of Alaska, p. 37.

In 1741, Behring's second expedition, which sailed from Okhotsk, resulted in the discovery of the American coast.

Ibid., pp. 62–74.

1741.

Unsatisfactory as the voyages of Behring and his associate Chirikoff undoubtedly were from a geographical point of view, it was upon their results that Russia chiefly based her subsequent

---

* This work will be referred to throughout these pages by the short title of "Alaska."

For the period discussed in this Chapter reference may be made generally to "Lyman's Diplomacy of the United States," 2nd edition, Boston, 1828, vol ii, chapter XI.

1741.		pretensions to the ownership of the north-western part of North America.
Hunters and traders followed Behring's lead, and Behring Island, and various islands of the Aleutian chain, were visited from the Kamtchatkan coast.
	Alaska, p. 141.	In 1763, Glottof, on a trading voyage, ventured as far east as Kadiak Island.
1768.	Ibid., pp. 157, 159.	In 1764 to 1768, Synd, a Lieutenant of the Russian navy, made an expedition along the coast to Behring Strait.
1769.		Of the period from 1769 to 1779, Bancroft writes in his History of Alaska:—
	Ibid., p. 174.	"From this time to the visit of Captain Cook, single traders and small Companies continued to traffic with the islands in much the same manner as before, though a general tendency to consolidation was perceptible."
1774.	Ibid., pp. 194-197.	The extension of Russian influence did not pass unnoticed by Spain, and in 1774 Perez was dispatched from Mexico on a voyage of exploration, in which he reached the southern part of Alaska.
1775.	Ibid., p. 197.	In 1775, Heceta, also instructed by the Viceroy of Mexico, explored the coast of America as far north as the 57th or 58th degree of latitude, taking possession of that part of the continent in the name of Spain.
1778.	Cook, Voyage to the Pacific Ocean, 1776-1780, London, 1874.	In 1778, Captain Cook, sent by the English Government, reached the American coast of the North Pacific with two vessels.

In pursuance of his instructions, he explored the coast from about 44° of north latitude as far as the region of Prince William Sound and Cook River or Inlet, taking possession of the coasts there. At Cook Inlet he found evidence of Russian trade but no Russians. At Unalaska, one of the Aleutian Islands, he again heard of the Russians, and on the occasion of a second visit met Russian traders. From Unalaska he sailed eastward to Bristol Bay, landing and taking possession. From this he explored, and defined the position of the American coast northward as far as Icy Cape, beyond Behring Strait.

Cook was killed in the following winter at the Sandwich Islands, but his ships, under Clarke, returned in 1779 and made further explorations in Behring Sea and in the Arctic Ocean.

Under this expedition, and for the first time, the

main outlines of the north-western part of the Continent of America, and particularly those of the coast about Prince William Sound and Cook Inlet, with the eastern coast of Behring Sea, were correctly traced.

This expedition also opened up the trade by sea in furs from the north-western part of America to China.

Cook's surveys still remain in many cases the most authentic; and these, with other results of the expedition were published in full in 1784.

In 1779, another officially accredited Spanish expedition under Arteaga and Quadra, explored part of the coast northward from about latitude 55°, and westward to Mount St. Elias. Alaska, pp. 217–221.

In 1783, the first attempt was made, following Cook's discoveries, to establish a Russian trading post on the American mainland, at Prince William Sound. It ended disastrously. Ibid., p. 186.

For some years after this reverse only one small vessel was dispatched from Siberia for trading purposes; but in 1784, Shelikof visited Unalaska and reached Kadiak Island, with the intention of effecting a permanent occupation there. Ibid., p. 191.
Ibid., p. 224.

In 1785, Captain Hanna entered into the trade between the north-west coast of America and China, for which Captain Cook's expedition had shown the way. He made a second voyage in the following year, but appears to have confined his trading operations to the vicinity of the northern part of Vancouver Island. Other commercial adventurers were, however, practically contemporaneous with Hanna, and this year is an important one in connection with the whole region. Bancroft, History of the North-west Coast, vol. i, pp. 173, 174.*

The "Captain Cook" and "Experiment," from Bombay, traded at Nootka and at Prince William Sound. Alaska, p. 249.

An English vessel, the "Lark," Captain Peters, from Bengal viâ Malacca and Canton, after trading at Petropaulovsk in Kamtchatka, sailed for Copper Island with the supposed purpose, as alleged, of obtaining a cargo of copper there. She was wrecked on the Commander Islands. Sauer's account of Billing's expedition, London, 1802, pp. 279, 281.

In the same year, 1786, Portlock and Dixon, and Meares, arrived upon the American coast, and traded and explored far to the northward.

---

* This work will be referred to throughout these pages by the short title of "North-west Coast."

1778.

1779.

1783.

1785.

1786–1789.

1786–1789.		These voyages are important, because detailed accounts of both were published, in 1789 and 1790 respectively, while the voyages of other traders have generally not been recorded.
	"A voyage round the World, &c.," London, 1789.	Portlock and Dixon, who had sailed from London in 1785 in the "King George" and "Queen Charlotte," in 1786, first visited Cook Inlet, where they found a party of Russians encamped, but with no fixed establishment. Trade was carried on with the natives there, and subsequently at various other places on what is now the Alaskan coast, and several harbours were surveyed. In the following year, Portlock and Dixon returned to the vicinity of Prince William Sound, where they found Meares, who had spent the previous winter there. They subsequently called at a number of places on the Alaskan coast, as well as at ports now included in the coast line of British Columbia, making very substantial additions to geographical knowledge.
	Meares' voyages 1790. See also "Annual Register," 1790, vol. xxxii, p. 287.	Meares sailing from Bengal in the "Nootka" early in the year, reached the Islands of Atka and Amlia of the Aleutian chain, staying two days at the last-named island, and holding communication with the natives and Russians found there. He then proceeded eastward along the Aleutian Islands, and was piloted into Unalaska by a Russian who came off to the ship. He describes the Russian establishment as consisting of underground huts like those occupied by the natives; but being anxious to leave the vicinity of the Russian traders, he continued his voyage eastward to Cook Inlet and eventually wintered in Prince William Sound, as above stated.
		Meares' later voyage, in 1788 and 1789, which is better known than his first venture, was directed to that part of the coast lying to the southward of the limits afterwards included by the Ukase of 1799. In 1788, Meares built at Nootka, in the northern part of Vancouver Island, the first vessel ever constructed on the coast of the north-western part of America. She was intended for use in the fur trade, and was appropriately named the "North-West America."
1786.	Alaska, p. 253.	Also in 1786, La Pérouse, on his voyage round the world, under instructions of the French Government, first made the American land near

Mount St. Elias. Thence he sailed eastward and southward, calling at places on the Alaskan coast. At Lituya Bay he obtained in trade 1,000 sea-otter skins. Alaska, p. 243. 1786.

In the same year the Russian Pribyloff discovered the islands in Behring Sea, now known by his name. Ibid., pp. 192-193.

In 1788, a Spanish expedition, in the vessels "Princesa" and "San Carlos," under Martinez and Haro, set out. It visited Prince William Sound, but found no Russians. Haro, however, found a Russian colony at Three Saints, on Kadiak Island. This was the easternmost place which had at this time a permanent Russian settlement. The voyagers took possession of Unalaska for Spain, but afterwards found Russian traders on the island. Ibid., pp. 270-272. 1788.

1788.

In the same year, a Russian vessel explored Prince William Sound, Yakutat, and Lituya Bays, all of which had previously been examined by English or French voyagers. Ibid., pp. 267-270.

In 1788, vessels from the United States first traded on the north-west coast. North-west Coast, vol. i, p. 185.

Upon the conflict of interests at this time along this part of the American coast, and the rival claims to territory there, Bancroft makes the following remarks:—

"The events of 1787-88 must have been puzzling to the natives of Prince William Sound. Englishmen under the English flag, Englishmen under the Portuguese flag, Spaniards and Russians, were cruizing about, often within a few miles of each other, taking possession, for one nation or the other, of all the land in sight." Alaska, p. 267.

Referring to Billing's Russian scientific exploring expedition, by which several voyages were made from 1787 to 1791 in the Behring Sea region, Bancroft says:—

"The geographical results may be set down at next to nothing, with the exception of the thorough surveys of Captain Bay in Illiuliuk Harbour on Unalaska Island. Every other part of the work had already been done by Cook." Ibid., p. 296.

The complaints of natives, against the practices of independent traders and adventurers, brought back by this expedition, had much to do with the subsequent grant of a monopoly of the trade to the Russian-American Company.

1789.	North west Coast, vol. i, pp. 204-212.	In 1789, twelve vessels at least are known to have been trading on the north-west coast.*
		The well-known "Nootka" seizures by the Spaniards occurred in this year.
1790.	Alaska, p. 273.	In 1790, Fidalgo sailed from Nootka, then occupied by Spain, to examine the north-west coast, including Prince William Sound, Cook
	Ibid., p. 325.	Inlet, and Kadiak. The trading-vessel "Phœnix," Captain Moore, from the East Indies, was in Prince William Sound in this year.
	Ibid., p. 285.	At this time also, Russia and Sweden being at war, a Swedish cruizer visited the Aleutian Islands, but finding no Government establishment to attack, and no Russians except traders living "in abject misery," her Commander refrained from disturbing them.
1791.	Ibid., p. 274.	In 1791, Malaspina, from Spain, under orders of his Government, visited several places upon what is now the Alaskan coast. Marchand, in
	Ibid., p. 275.	the " Solide," from France, on a voyage of trade and circumnavigation, also visited the coast, and
	Ibid., p. 248.	Douglas, in the " Iphigenia," was in Cook Inlet in this year.
	North-west Coast, vol. i, pp. 250-257.	Besides the above vessels, at least eight trading-vessels are known to have been on the coast, of which seven were from the United States.
1792.	Alaska, p. 244.	In 1792, Caamano, setting out from Nootka, explored Port Bucarelli, in South-eastern Alaska; and it is reported that in this year fully twenty-eight vessels were upon the coast, at least half of them being engaged in the fur trade.
	Vancouver, vol. iii, p. 498. Voyage of Discovery to the Pacific Ocean. London, 1798.	Vancouver gives a list of 21 vessels for the same year, divided as follows: From England, 6; from East Indies, 2; from China, 3; from United States, 7; from Portugal, 2; from France, 1.
	Alaska, p. 296.	The "Halcyon," Captain Barclay, visited Petropaulovsk for purposes of trade, and a French vessel, " La Flavia," wintered there.
1793.	Vancouver's voyage.	In 1793, Vancouver, who had been dispatched by the English Government with the "Discovery" and "Chatham" for the purpose of

* In many cases no records exist of the trading voyages made to the north-west coast, and the existing records are very incomplete. It is in some cases certainly known that these traders extended their operations to the north of the limit mentioned in the Ukase of 1799, or that of the Ukase of 1821. In other cases the extent of the voyages made is unknown. The traders went, in fact, wherever skins could be purchased, and, if disappointed or forestalled at one place, at once departed for another. None of these trading-vessels were Russian.

finally deciding the existence or otherwise of a communication between the Pacific and Atlantic, by the exploration of all remaining inlets on the north-west coast, was occupied in surveying operations on what now constitutes the south-eastern Alaskan coast. 1793.

In 1794, he surveyed Cook Inlet to its head, and Prince William Sound, Kadiak, and the coast extending to Yakutat Bay, were in turn carefully laid down in detail. He ascertained that the easternmost Russian Establishment at this time was at Port Etches on Prince William Sound. *Vancouver's voyage.* 1794.

Concerning the Russians here and there met with, Vancouver remarks that he— *Ibid., vol. iii, p. 199.*

"clearly understood that the Russian Government had little to do with these Settlements; that they were solely under the direction and support of independent mercantile Companies. . . . Not the least attention whatever is paid to the cultivation of the land or to any other object but that of collecting furs, which is principally done by the Indians."

Near Yakutat Bay he fell in with the "Jackal," an English trading-vessel, which was then upon the coast for the third consecutive season; and further to the south-eastward he met with the "Arthur," Captain Barber, from Bengal.

Vancouver took possession of the coast southward from Cross Sound (latitude 58°) in the name of Great Britain. The results of his surveys were published in 1798.

The names of four trading-vessels on the north-west coast, including the "Jackal," are known for this year. *North-west Coast, vol. i, p. 297.*

In 1795, a trading-vessel, named the "Phœnix," from Bengal, was on the north-west coast. *Ibid., p. 304.* 1795.

In 1796, at least three trading-vessels are known to have been on the north-west coast. *Ibid., p. 305.* 1796.

In 1797, the names of four trading-vessels on this coast are known, but these constituted probably but a small part of the fleet. *Ibid., p. 306.* 1797.

In 1798, the names of six trading-vessels happen to have been recorded. *Ibid., vol. i, p. 306.* 1798.

In 1799, the "Caroline," Captain Cleveland, from Boston, arrived at Sitka shortly after a Russian post had been established there. 1799.

Several other American vessels, among them the brig "Eliza," under Captain Rowan, visited Sitka during the summer and "absorbed the trade *Alaska, p. 389.*

1709.		while the Russians were preparing to occupy the field in the future."
	North-west Coast, vol. I, p. 307.	The names of seven vessels trading on the north-west coast are recorded in this year.

Nothing approaching to a complete record of the names or nationalities of vessels trading upon this part of the coast in the years about the close of the last century can now be obtained, and, in the absence of any published record of explorations, even incidental allusions to the presence of such traders become rare in the years after the date of Vancouver's departure. That such trade was, however, continuously practised is evident from the general complaints made by the Russians as to its effect on their operations.

The following quotations from Bancroft's "History of Alaska" allude to complaints referring particularly to those years.

Writing of the enterprises of Baranoff, Governor of Sitka, Bancroft says:—

1798–1801.	Alaska, p. 384.	"At every point eastward of Kadiak where he had endeavoured to open trade, he found himself forestalled by English and American ships, which had raised the prices of skins almost beyond his limited means."

Again, referring specially to the nascent Establishment at Sitka, Baranoff himself writes:—

	Ibid., p. 395.	"I thought there would be no danger with proper protection from the larger vessels, though the natives there possess large quantities of fire-arms and all kinds of ammunition, receiving new supplies annually from the English and from the Republicans of Boston and America, whose object is not permanent settlement on these shores, but who have been in the habit of making trading trips to these regions."

On another page Bancroft writes:—

	Ibid., p. 398.	"Baranoff's complaints of foreign encroachment appear to have been well grounded. Within a few leagues of Sitka the captains of three Boston ships secured 2,000 skins, though paying very high prices, each one trying to outbid the other."

	Ibid., p. 399.	Further on Baranoff is quoted to the effect that the Americans had been acquainted with the tribes in this region for two or three years, and sent there annually from six to eight vessels. These vessels from the United States were at this time just beginning to supplant the English traders, who had in earlier years been the more numerous.

Once more Bancroft quotes Baranoff as follows:—

"The resources of this region are such that millions may be made there for our country with proper management in the future, but for over ten years from six to ten English and American vessels have called here every year. It is safe to calculate an average of 2,000 skins on eight, or say six vessels, which would make 12,000 a-year, and if we even take 10,000 as a minimum, it would amount in ten years to 100,000 skins, which at the price at Canton of 45 roubles per skin, would amount to 4,500,000 roubles." *Alaska, p. 399.*

Circumstances which led up to Ukase of 1799.

It will be convenient at this point to consider the circumstances which led up to the Ukase of 1799, the terms of that Ukase, and its effect.

As early as 1786, the idea had become dominant with Grigor Shelikof, who had shortly before established the first permanent Russian colony at Kadiak, of creating a Company which should hold a monopoly of trade in the Russian possessions on the Pacific, and over all that part of the American Continent to which Russian traders resorted. Shelikof obtained but a partial success in the Charter issued for the United American Company; but after his death at Irkutsk in 1795, his schemes were taken up by his son-in-law Rezanof, who succeeded in carrying them to completion, and, in 1799, a Ukase was issued which granted the wished-for exclusive privileges to the new Russian-American Company. Before this time, in 1798, a consolidation of the Shelikof Company with several smaller concerns had been effected under the name of the United American Company; and at the date of the issuing of the Ukase there were but two rival Companies of importance in the field, the Shelikof or United American Company, and the Lebedef Company, and these engaged in active competition and hostility. *Alaska, p. 303.* *Ibid., pp. 377–379.*

Bancroft sums up the situation about 1791 and 1792 in the following words:—

"Affairs were assuming a serious aspect. Not only were the Shelikof men luled from the greater part of the inlet [Cook Inlet], but they were opposed in their advance round Prince William Sound, which was also claimed by the Lebedef faction, though the Orekhof and other Companies were hunting there . . . . *Ibid., pp. 338 339.*

Circumstances which led up to Ukase of 1799.

"Thus the history of Cook Inlet during the last decade of the eighteenth century is replete with romantic incidents—midnight raids, ambuscades, and open warfare—resembling the doings of mediæval *raubritters*, rather than the exploits of peaceable traders....

"Robbery and brutal outrages continued to be the order of the day, though now committed chiefly for the purpose of obtaining sole control of the inlet, to the neglect of legitimate pursuits."

Again, in another place, the same author writes, with regard especially to the position of Baranoff, Governor of Sitka, when he took charge of the Shelikof Colony of Kadiak:—

Alaska, p. 321.

"Thus, on every side, rival establishments and traders were draining the country of the valuable staple upon which rested the very existence of the scheme of colonization. To the east and north there were Russians, but to the south-east the ships of Englishmen, Americans, and Frenchmen were already traversing the tortuous channels of the Alexander Archipelago, reaping rich harvests of sea-otter skins, in the very region where Baranoff had decided to extend Russian dominion in connection with Company sway."

Ibid., pp. 202, 391, 393.

It was only in the later years of the competition between the rival Russian Companies that they began to assume hostile attitudes to one another. The growing power of some of them favoured aggression, and the increasing scarcity of the sea-otter, which was already beginning to be felt, accentuated it. At first, and for many years after Behring's initial voyage, the traders from Siberia were sufficiently occupied in turning to advantage their dealings with the natives of the islands and coasts visited by them, and this not in the most scrupulous manner. Tribute in furs was exacted from the Aleuts on various pretexts, and whenever the traders came in sufficient force these people were virtually enslaved. Not only were the companies of traders under no sufficient or recognized control by the Russian Government, but they even disliked and resented in some measure the advent or presence among them of commissioned officers of the Government.

Ibid., p. 301.

The effect of the reports of the subordinate members of Billing's expedition, as to the unsatisfactory state of affairs in the Aleutian Islands and on the American coast, tended to favour the project of the establishment of a monopoly, by disclosing the abuses which existed by reason of the existing competition. Bancroft more than hints that the superior officers of the expedition

Ibid., p. 299.

were induced to keep silence from interested motives; and Billing's Report, whatever its tenour may have been, was never published.

In the end, however, it became in a degree imperative for the Russian Government to put a stop to the scandals and abuses which flourished in this remote and practically uncontrolled portion of the Empire, and the easiest way in which this could be done, and the least expensive, was to vest exclusive rights in the hands of the most powerful of the existing rival Companies. This, being also in the interests of the Company in question, was not found difficult of achievement, and, as a consequence of the Ukase of 1799, the absorption of the smaller concerns still existing appears to have followed without any great difficulty, Baranoff, as the executive head of the new Corporation on the American coast, coming to the front as the natural leader.

When Shelikof presented at St. Petersburg his original petition for the right to monopolize the trade, a Report was requested on the subject from Jacobi, the Governor-General of Eastern Siberia, and in Jacobi, Shelikof found an able advocate. Jacobi stated that it would be only just to Shelikof to grant his request, and that it would be unfair to allow others to enjoy the benefits of the peace which Shelikof had established at Kadiak.

The Empress then ordered the Imperial College of Commerce to examine the question, and a Committee of this body endorsed Jacobi's Report and recommended that the request of Shelikof and Golikof for exclusive privileges should be granted.

Though, among the arguments naturally advanced in favour of the grant of a monopoly, we find it urged that the benefits of trade accruing would thus be reserved to Russian subjects, the history of the occupation of the coasts and the records concerning it, show conclusively that this was not the object which to any great extent induced Shelikof to apply for such a monopoly. His Company had the utmost difficulty in sustaining its position against hostile natives, while not less serious were the difficulties arising from the competition, and scarcely veiled hostility of rival Russian traders. The increasing trade by foreigners, together with the numerous exploring and surveying expeditions dispatched

Circumstances which led up to Ukase of 1799.

Alaska, p. 308.

Ibid., p. 702.

Circumstances which led up to Ukase of 1799.	to the north-west coast of America by various Powers, were no doubt distrusted by the Russian traders; but at the same time these traders were often obliged to depend on such foreigners for support and assistance. Nowhere in the annals of the times previous to, and during the operation of the Ukase of 1799, do we find any reference to attempts to interfere with or restrict the operations of foreigners upon the American coasts or in the Aleutian Islands. Even the scientific expeditions of the period were often largely interested in trade as well as in exploration, but all vessels meeting with the Russians report a favourable, if not a hospitable reception. Such an attitude on the part of the traders and the Company is, in fact, strictly in accord with the Ukase of 1799, which is purely domestic in its character, and in which no exclusive rights against foreigners are asserted.

Ukase of 1799.

Text of Ukase of 1799.	The following is a literal translation of the Ukase in question, taken from Golovnin, in "Materialni dla Istoriy Russkikh Zasseleniy," i. 77-80:—
Alaska, pp. 379-380.	"By the grace of a merciful God, we, Paul I, Emperor and Autocrat of All the Russians, &c. To the Russian-American Company, under our highest protection, the benefits and advantages resulting to our Empire from the hunting and trading carried on by our loyal subjects in the north-eastern seas and along the coasts of America have attracted our Royal attention and consideration; therefore, having taken under our immediate protection a Company organized for the above-named purpose of carrying on hunting and trading, we allow it to assume the appellation of 'Russian-American Company under our highest protection;' and for the purpose of aiding the Company in its enterprises, we allow the Commanders of our land and sea forces to employ said forces in the Company's aid if occasion requires it, while for further relief and assistance of said Company, and having examined their Rules and Regulations, we hereby declare it to be our highest Imperial will to grant to this Company for a period of twenty years the following rights and privileges:— "1. By the right of discovery in past times by Russian navigators of the north-eastern part of America, beginning from the 55th degree of north latitude and of the chain of islands extending from Kamschatka to the north to America and southward to Japan, and by right of possession of the same by Russia, we most graciously permit the Company to have the use of all hunting grounds and

establishments now existing on the north-eastern [*sic*] coast of America, from the above-mentioned 55th degree to Behring Strait, and on the same also on the Aleutian, Kurile, and other islands situated in the north-eastern ocean.

"2. To make new discoveries not only north of the 55th degree of north latitude but farther to the south, and to occupy the new lands discovered as Russian possessions, according to prescribed rules, if they have not been previously occupied by any other nation, or been dependent on another nation.

"3. To use and profit by everything which has been or shall be discovered in those localities, on the surface and in the bosom of the earth, without any competition by others.

"4. We most graciously permit this Company to establish Settlements in future times, wherever they are wanted, according to their best knowledge and belief, and fortify them to insure the safety of the inhabitants, and to send ships to those shores with goods and hunters, without any obstacles on the part of the Government.

"5. To extend their navigation to all adjoining nations and hold business intercourse with all surrounding Powers, upon obtaining their free consent for the purpose, and under our highest protection, to enable them to prosecute their enterprises with greater force and advantage.

"6. To employ for navigation, hunting, and all other business, free, and unsuspected people, having no illegal views or intentions. In consideration of the distance of the localities where they will be sent, the provincial authorities will grant to all persons sent out as settlers, hunters, and in other capacities, passports for seven years. Serfs and house-servants will only be employed by the Company with the consent of their land-holders, and Government taxes will be paid for all serfs thus employed.

"7. Though it is forbidden by our highest order to cut Government timber anywhere without the permission of the College of Admiralty, this Company is hereby permitted, on account of the distance of the Admiralty from Okhotsk, when it needs timber for repairs, and occasionally for the construction of new ships, to use freely such timber as is required.

"8. For shooting animals, for marine signals, and on all unexpected emergencies on the mainland of America and on the islands, the Company is permitted to buy for cash, at cost price, from the Government artillery magazine at Irkutsk yearly 40 or 50 pouds of powder, and from the Nertchinsk mine 200 pouds of lead.

"9. If one of the partners of the Company becomes indebted to the Government or to private persons, and is not in a condition to pay them from any other property except what he holds in the Company, such property cannot be seized for the satisfaction of such debts, but the debtor shall not be permitted to use anything but the interest or dividends of such property until the term of the Company's privileges expires, when it will be at his or his creditors' disposal.

"10. The exclusive right most graciously granted to the

Text of Ukase of 1799.

Text of Ukase of 1799.

Company for a period of twenty years, to use and enjoy, in the above-described extent of country and islands, all profits and advantages derived from hunting, trade, industries, and discovery of new lands, prohibiting the enjoyment of those profits and advantages not only to those who would wish to sail to those countries on their own account, but to all former hunters and trappers who have been engaged in this trade, and have their vessels and furs at those places; and other Companies which may have been formed will not be allowed to continue their business unless they unite with the present Company with their free consent; but such private Companies or traders as have their vessels in those regions can either sell their property, or, with the Company's consent, remain until they have obtained a cargo, but no longer than is required for the loading and return of their vessel; and after that nobody will have any privileges but this one Company, which will be protected in the enjoyment of all the advantages mentioned.

"11. Under our highest protection, the Russian-American Company will have full control over all above-mentioned localities, and exercise judicial powers in minor cases. The Company will also be permitted to use all local facilities for fortifications in the defence of the country under their control against foreign attacks. Only partners of the Company shall be employed in the administration of the new possessions in charge of the Company.

"In conclusion of this our most gracious order for the benefit of the Russian-American Company under highest protection, we enjoin all our military and civil authorities in the above-mentioned localities not only not to prevent them from enjoying to the fullest extent the privileges granted by us, but in case of need to protect them with all their power from loss or injury, and to render them, upon application of the Company's authorities, all necessary aid, assistance, and protection.

"To give effect to this our most gracious Order, we subscribe it with our own hand, and give orders to confirm it with our Imperial seal.

"Given at St. Petersburgh, in the year after the birth of Christ 1799, the 27th day of December, in the fourth year of our reign.

(Signed) "PAUL."

The Ukase of 1799 considered.

The Ukase, it will be observed, granted to the Russian-American Company exclusive rights as against other Russian subjects only, and in no way interfered with the rights of foreigners, notwithstanding that the representations which led to its promulgation contained, as has already been indicated, complaints of competition by foreigners.

It will be noticed, for instance, that the details incorporated in clause 10 of the Ukase respecting the rights of independent traders are such as to be applicable to Russian subjects or Companies alone.

The rights and privileges under the grant

extended to the hunting grounds and establishments then existing on the main coast of America from Behring Strait down to the 55th degree of north latitude.

The southern limit of the exclusive coast privileges granted to the Company extended on the Asiatic side to Japan.

Not only were the main coasts of Asia and America thus covered by the Ukase, but the same privileges were granted on the Aleutian, Kurile, and other islands "situated in the North-Eastern Ocean."

It will be noted, therefore, that the area over which the exclusive privileges were granted to the Russian-American Company extended both on the coast of Asia and of America far beyond the limits of Behring Sea.

Special privileges in regard to the purchase of powder for shooting animals " on the mainland of America and on the islands " were conceded, and the exclusive right " to use and enjoy in the above-described extent of country and islands " the hunting and trading.

The Ukase in no way claimed any exclusive jurisdiction over the sea, nor were any measures taken under it to restrict the commerce, navigation, or fishery of the subjects of foreign nations, and this although, within the very area covered by the Ukase, as has already been shown by the facts stated, vessels of various nations had been navigating and trading.

The Ukase of 1799 purely domestic.

It will be seen, by the account of the years following 1799, that these operations on the part of foreigners continued.

Referring to the Ukase of 1799, Mr. Middleton, the United States' Minister at St. Petersburgh, writes, 7th (19th) April, 1824, to Mr. Adams, the Secretary of State of the United States, as follows:—

"The confusion prevailing in Europe in 1799 permitted Russia (who alone seems to have kept her attention fixed upon this interest during that period) to take a decided step towards the monopoly of this trade, by the Ukase of that date, which trespassed upon the acknowedged rights of Spain;* but at that moment the Emperor Paul had declared war against that country as being an ally of

American State Papers, Foreign Relations, vol. v, p. 461.

---

* The rights of Spain are here mentioned because, by the Ukase of 1799, Russia claimed territory which Spain was also understood to claim. In 1824 the United States was committed in its own interest to support the old Spanish claim, in consequence of the Spanish cession to the United States in 1819.

29

France. This Ukase which is, in its *form*, an act purely domestic, was never notified to any foreign State with injunction to respect its provisions. Accordingly, it appears to have been passed over unobserved by foreign Powers, and it remained without execution in so far as it militated against their rights."

Historical outline resumed.

The accuracy of the views expressed by Mr. Middleton appears clearly from the facts disclosed by the chronological statement relating to the period subsequent to the year 1799:—

Alaska, p. 389.

In 1800, the ship "Enterprise," from New York, arrived at Kadiak.

North-west Coast, vol. i, p. 308.

The name of seven trading-vessels on the north-west coast are given in this year.

Ibid., p. 310.
Robert Greenhow, Librarian of United States' Department of State. "History of Oregon and California," pp 266, 267.
North American Review, 1822, Article XVIII.
See Appendix, vol. i, No. 3.

In 1801, there were at least thirteen United States' vessels on the north-west coast. These vessels exchanged with the natives of the coast for furs parts of their cargoes, and, proceeding to China, returned to their respective countries with cargoes of teas, &c. Upwards of 18,000 sea-otter skins, besides other furs, were in 1801 collected by United States' traders alone for the China market.

In 1802, the Russian Establishment at Sitka was destroyed, and nearly all the Russians there were massacred by the natives. According to Lisiansky, the natives were assisted by three deserters from a United States' vessel, the "Jenny," which had called at Sitka not long

Alaska, pp. 404–409.

before. Shortly afterwards, an English vessel, the "Unicorn," Captain Barber, arrived at Sitka, and two other vessels, reported by the Russian survivors as English, but one of these Bancroft believes to have been the United States' vessel "Alert."

In this year also Kruseustern, having visited China, presented a Memorial to the Russian Government calling attention to the advantages offered by the trade in furs from America direct to Chinese ports, and suggesting that Russia should engage in it.

North-west Coast, vol. i, pp. 311 312.

Of the vessels trading on the north-west coast in this year, the names of ter. have been recorded.

Ibid., p. 117.

In 1803, Baranoff contemplated the abandonment of Unalaska, owing to disease and non-arrival of supplies. He ordered that the best men should be moved to the Pribyloff Islands to collect there the furs accumulated by the natives. These islands had not been visited for many years.

Captain O'Cain, of the United States' vessel "O'Cain," exchanged goods for furs with Baranoff at Sitka, and also took Aleutian hunters to the Californian coast to hunt fur-seals and sea-otters. "Thus was inaugurated a series of hunting expeditions beyond the borders of the Russian Colonies, which continued for many years." [Alaska, pp. 477, 478]

The names of five vessels trading on the north-west coast are known. [North-west Coast, vol. i, pp. 312-317.]

1803.

In 1804, Sitka was reoccupied and rebuilt by the Russians. Two United States' vessels, one being the "Juno," were there. The names of four vessels are known as trading on the north-west coast. [Ibid., pp. 318, 219.]

1804.

In 1805, the "Juno" and another vessel from the United States were at Sitka, and we hear of six vessels, including the "Juno," as trading on the north-west coast. [Ibid., p. 320.]

1805.

In 1806, the Russian Envoy Rezanoff visited the Pribyloff Islands on the "Maria," and endeavoured to stop the wasteful slaughter of fur-seals. He recommended the Emperor to "take a stronger hold of the country," as the traders in ships from Boston were undermining the trade with China. He reported that the "Bostonians" had armed the Kolosh Indians. [Alaska, p. 446.] [Ibid., p. 451.]

In the same year the "Juno," with her cargo, was purchased by Baranoff, and the "Eclipse" (Captain O'Cain) sailed for China with furs, but was lost on the way back. [Ibid., p. 454.] [Ibid., pp. 478, 479.]

The names of four vessels trading on the north-west coast are known in this year.

Rezanoff, in 1807, sent the "Juno" to the Californian coast for provisions. The "Myrtle," an English ship (Captain Barber), was purchased by Baranoff. Six north-west coast trading-vessels are known by name for this year. [Ibid., p. 461.]

1807.

In 1808, the United States' vessel "Mercury" obtained at Kadiak 25 bidarkas, or skin-boats, for hunting and trading to the southward. [Ibid., pp. 479, 480.]

1808.

Four United States' trading-vessels are known to have been on the Alaskan coast in 1808 and 1809.

1809

1810.	Alaska, p. 467.	In 1810, the Russian sloop-of-war "Diana" visited Sitka. There were several United States' vessels in the port at the time. Shortly after the United States' vessels "Enterprise" and "O'Cain" arrived. The "Enterprise" went to Canton with furs.
	Ibid., p. 470.	Golovnin, Commander of the "Diana," writes that at this time an American sailor and a Prussian skipper composed the Diplomatic Corps of the Russian-American Company.
	North-west Coast, vol. i, p. 325.	In 1810 and 1811, four foreign vessels were engaged in sea-otter hunting, under Russian contracts.
1811.	Alaska, p. 429.	In 1811, the "Enterprise" returned from and went back to China with furs. In this year the Ross Colony was founded in California to provide agricultural products for use on the northwest coast. Five vessels engaged in trading and hunting, besides the four vessels under Russian contracts, were seen on the coast of Southern Alaska in this year.
	Ibid., p. 483.	
	North-west Coast, vol. i, p. 326.	
	Alaska, p. 472.	In 1812, the United States' ship "Beaver" disposed of her cargo to Baranoff at Sitka, and was then sent to the Pribyloff Islands for fur-seal skins as payment.
	Ibid. p. 480.	Between 1800 and 1812, Baranoff made six additional hunting contracts with United States' vessels. He received a proportion of the skins, which were chiefly sea-otters.
1812.	North-west Coast, vol. i, p. 329.	Between 1812 and 1814, there was scarcely any trade, owing to the war between England and the United States.
1814.	Alaska, p. 503.	In 1814, Captain Bennett (United States) sold two vessels with their cargoes to Baranoff, and took fur-seal skins from the Pribyloff Islands in payment. Lozaref, sent by Russia, with two ships, reached Sitka, but quarrelled with Baranoff and returned.
	Ibid., pp. 504, 505.	
1815.	Ibid. p. 506.	In 1815, the Russian vessel "Isabel" reached Sitka with Dr. Sheffer on board.
1816.	Ibid., p. 507.	In 1816, the Russian vessel "Rurik" (Captain Kotzebue) touched at St. Lawrence Island and explored Kotzebue Sound, north of Behring Strait.
	North-west Coast, vol. i, p. 335.	Two United States' vessels visited the Russian Settlements this year.
1817		In 1817, Kotzebue, on an exploring expedition to the North, only reached St. Lawrence Island.
	Alaska, p. 510.	An expedition in two vessels under Hagemeister, sent by Russia, reached Sitka.

In 1818, Hagemeister superseded Baranoff, under instructions. Roquefeuil, a French officer, arrived at Sitka in the "Bordelais," a trading-vessel. He sailed for Prince of Wales Archipelago, but had a conflict with natives and returned to Sitka. Roquefeuil notes meeting a United States' and a British trading-vessel in Alaskan waters.

Alaska, pp. 522, 523.

North-west Coast, vol. i, p. 338.

1818.

In 1818 and 1821, expeditions were dispatched by the British Government in seach of a north-west passage from the Atlantic to the Pacific. These efforts were continued, and in 1824 and 1825 Parry, Beechey, and Franklin were engaged in the same quest, Beechey having been directed to pass through Behring Strait and to rendezvous with the others at Kotzebue Sound. These efforts were stimulated by the offer by Parliament of large pecuniary awards, and it is obvious that the value of the discovery, if made, depended on the free right of navigation for purposes of commerce through Behring Strait.

Encyclopædia Britannica, 9th ed., vol. xix, p. 319.

In 1819, the United States' traders obtained most of the trade, bartering with the Kolosh fire-arms and rum for skins. They obtained about 8,000 skins a-year. The Russians could not successfully compete with them.

Alaska, p. 528.

1819.

The privileges granted for twenty years to the Russian-American Company were now about to expire, and Golovnin was instructed to inquire as to its operations. His Report was not favourable.

He writes:—

"Three things are wanting, in the organization of the Company's colonies: a clearer definition of the duties belonging to the various officers, a distinction of rank, and a regular uniform, so that foreigners visiting these parts may see something indicating the existence of forts and troops belonging to the Russian sceptre — something resembling a regular garrison. At present they can come to no other conclusion than that these stations are but temporary fortifications erected by hunters as a defence against savages."

Ibid., p. 531.

In 1820, four trading-vessels are known to have been operating on the north-west coast.

North-west Coast, vol. i, p. 340.

1820.

The extent of Russian occupation at about the date of the expiry of the first Charter can be shown by the Census taken in 1819, which states the number of Russians as follows:—

Alaska, p. 522.

		Men.	Women.
For Tikhmeneff's complete Tables, including natives, see Appendix, vol. , No. 3.	Sitka, or New Archangel	198	11
	Kadiak and adjoining Islands	73	..
	Island of Ookamok	2	..
	Katmai	4	..
	Sutkhumokoi	3	..
	Voskressensky Harbour	2	..
	Fort Constantine	17	..
	Nikolai, Cook Inlet	11	..
	Alexandrovsk, Cook Inlet	11	..
	Ross Settlement, California	27	..
	Seal Islands	27	..
	Nushagak [the only Settlement on the continent north of the Aleutian Islands]	3	2
	Total	378	13

Uncertainty of territorial claims in 1818.

See also Adams to Rush, July 22, 1823; American State Papers, Foreign Relations, vol. v, p. 440; and also Confidential Memorial inclosed in letter, Middleton to Adams, December 1 (15), 1823; American State Papers, Foreign Relations, vol. v, p. 449. See Appendix, vol. ii, Part II, Nos. 4 and 5. For text of Convention, see American State Papers, vol. iv, p. 406.

While the subjects of Russia, Spain, Great Britain and the United States were doubtless making claims on the part of their respective countries from time to time, so uncertain were these claims and the merits of each, that in 1818 (20th October), in the Convention between the United States and Great Britain, it was agreed that any—

"country that may be claimed by either party on the north-west coast of America, westward of the Stony Mountains, shall, together with its harbours, bays, and creeks, and the navigation of all rivers within the same, be free and open for the term of ten years from the date of the signature of the present Convention, to the vessels, citizens, and subjects of the two Powers, it being well understood that this agreement is not to be construed to the prejudice of any claim which either of the two High Contracting Parties may have to any part of the said country, nor shall it be taken to affect the claims of any other Power or State to any part of the said country, the only object of the High Contracting Parties in that respect being to prevent disputes and differences amongst themselves."

Russian territorial claim in 1821.

American State Papers, Foreign Relations, vol. v, p. 436.

See Appendix, vol. ii, Part II, No. 3.

Mr. Adams, Secretary of State of the United States, in a despatch to Mr. Middleton, the United States' Minister at St. Petersburgh, dated 22nd July, 1823, contended that even as late as that year Russian rights in the region under consideration "were confined to certain *islands* north of the 55th degree of latitude," and had "no existence on the continent of America."

In the same letter Mr. Adams observed :—

"It does not appear that there ever has been a permanent Russian Settlement on this continent south of latitude 59°, that of New Archangel, cited by M. Poletica, in latitude 57° 30', being upon an island. So far as prior *discovery* can constitute a foundation of right, the papers which I have referred to prove that it belongs to the United States as far as 59° north, by the transfer to them of the rights of Spain. There is, however, no part of the globe where the mere fact of discovery could be held to give weaker claims than on the north-west coast. 'The great sinuosity,' says Humboldt, 'formed by the coast between the 55th and 60th parallels of latitude, embraces discoveries made by Gali, Bering, and Tchivikoff, Quadra, Cook, La Pérouse, Malaspina, and Vancouver. No European nation has yet formed an establishment upon the immense extent of coast from Cape Mendosino to the 59th degree of latitude. Beyond that limit the Russian factories commence, most of which are scattered and distant from each other like the factories established by the European nations for the last three centuries on the coast of Africa. Most of these little Russian Colonies communicate with each other only by sea, and the new denominations of Russian-America or Russian possessions in the new continent, must not lead us to believe that the coast of Bering Bay, the Peninsula of Alaska, or the country of the Ischugatschi, have become Russian *provinces* in the same sense given to the word when speaking of the Spanish Provinces of Sonora, or New Biscay.' (Humboldt's ' New Spain,' vol. ii, Book 3, chap. 8, p. 496.)

"In M. Poletica's letter of the 28th February, 1822, to me, he says that when the Emperor Paul I granted to the present American Company its first Charter in 1799, he gave it the *exclusive possession* of the north-west coast of America, which belonged to Russia, from the 55th degree of north latitude, to Bering Strait.

"In his letter of 2nd April, 1822, he says that the Charter to the Russian-American Company in 1799, was merely conceding to them a part of the sovereignty, *or rather certain exclusive privileges of commerce.*

"This is the most corrrect view of the sub ect. The Emperor Paul granted to the Russian-American Company certain exclusive privileges of commerce — exclusive with reference to other Russian subjects; but Russia had never before *asserted* a right of sovereignty over any part of the North American continent; and in 1799 the people of the United States had been at least for twelve years in the constant and uninterrupted enjoyment of a profitable trade with the natives of that very coast, of which the Ukase of the Emperor Paul could not deprive them."

The Honourable Charles Sumner, speaking in the United States' Senate on the occasion of the cession of Alaska to the United States, in 1867, said:—

"It seems that there were various small Companies, of which that at Kadiak was the most considerable, all of which were finally fused into one large trading Company, known as the Russian-American Company, which was organized in 1799, under a Charter from the Emperor Paul, with the power of administration throughout the whole region, including the coasts and the islands. In this respect it was not unlike the East India Company,

Russian territorial claim in 1821.

H. R., Ex Doc. 177, 2nd Sess., 40th Cong., p. 149, 1867-68. See Appendix, vol. i, No. 6.

which has played such a part in English history; but it may be more properly compared with the Hudson Bay Company, of which it was a Russian counterpart. The Charter was for a term of years, but it has been from time to time extended, and, as I understand, is now on the point of expiring. The powers of the Company are sententiously described by the 'Almanach de Gotha' for 1867, where, under the head of Russia, it says that 'to the present t ie Russian America has been the *property of a Company*'

And, referring to as late a period as 1867, he remarked:—

Extent of Russian Settlements.

"It is evident that those Russian Settlements, distributed through an immense region, and far from any civilized neighbourhood, have little in common with those of European nations elsewhere, unless we except those of Denmark, on the west coast of Greenland. Nearly all are on the coast or the islands. They are nothing but 'villages' or 'factories' under the protection of palisades. Sitka is an exception, due unquestionably to its selection as the head-quarters of the Government, and also to the eminent character of the Governors who have made it their home."

Article XVIII, North American Review, vol. xv, Quarterly Review, 1821-22, vol xxvi. See Appendix, vol. i, Nos. 3 and 4.

Touching Russia's claims to exclusive jurisdiction over more than certain islands in the Pacific Ocean on the American coast, Mr. Adams, moreover, in 1823 brought forward with approval, articles which appeared in "The North American Review," published in the United States, and in the "Quarterly Review," published in England. The facts stated in these articles show the grounds upon which the Government of the United States considered themselves justified in the contention advanced by Mr. Adams, that "the rights of discovery, of occupancy, of uncontested possession," alleged by Russia, were "all without foundation in fact," as late as the year 1823.

Adams to Middleton, July 22, 1823. See Appendix, vol. ii, Part II, No. 3.

Again referring to the circumstances in the year 1867 (the date of the cession of Alaska to the United States), the historian Bancroft writes:—

Alaska, p. 591.

"Moreover, Russia had never occupied, and never wished to occupy, this territory. For two-thirds of a century she had been represented there, as we have seen, almost entirely by a fur and trading Company under the protection of Government. In a measure it had controlled, or endeavoured to control, the affairs of that Company, and among its stockholders were several members of the Royal Family; but Alaska had been originally granted to the Russian-American Company by Imperial Ukas, and by Imperial Oukas the Charter had been twice renewed. Now that the Company had declined to accept a fourth Charter on the terms proposed, something must be done with the territory, and Russia would lose no actual portion of her Empire in ceding it to a Republic with which she was on friendly terms, and whose domain seemed destined to spread over the entire continent."

The foregoing historical summary establishes—

That from the earliest periods of which any records exist down to the year 1821, there is no evidence that Russia either asserted or exercised in the non-territorial waters of the North Pacific any rights to the exclusion of other nations.

That during the whole of that period the shores of America and Asia belonging to Russia as far north as Behring Straits, and the waters lying between those coasts, as well as the islands therein, were visited by the trading-vessels of all nations, including those sailing under the flags of Great Britain, the United States, Spain, and France, with the knowledge of the Russian authorities.

That the only rights, in fact, exercised by Russia or on her behalf, were the ordinary territorial rights connected with settlements or annexations of territory consequent upon such settlements, and the only rights she purported to deal with or confer were rights and privileges given to the Russian-American Company, as Russian subjects, in preference over other Russian subjects.

CHAPTER II.

HEAD B.—*The Ukase of 1821, and the circumstances connected therewith leading up to the Treaties of 1824 and 1825.*

Ukase of 1821.

Voyage, M. de Krusenstern, vol. i, p. 14. American State Papers, Foreign Relations, vol. v, pp. 453, 454.

Competition by Foreigners.

American State Papers, vol. v, pp. 438–443. Alaska, p. 528. Tikhmenieff, Inter. Obos. I, cited in note to Alaska, p. 532.

See also Alaska, p. 446; Rezanof's complaint in 1806.

Shortly before the date of the renewal of the Charter of the Russian-American Company in 1821, the aspect of affairs had considerably changed.

The Company had long before fully succeeded in getting rid of its Russian rivals, but trading-vessels from England and from the United States frequented the coasts in increasing numbers, and everywhere competed with the Company. Goods were brought by these vessels at prices which the Company could not successfully meet, and furs were taken by them direct to Chinese sea-ports, while the Company, as a rule, had still to depend on the overland route from Okhotsk to Kiakhta on the Amoor.

Domestic competition had in fact ceased, and the most serious drawback to the success of the Company consisted in the competition from abroad.

The difficulties resulting to the Company on account of foreign competition appear prominently in the complaints made by its agents at this time, and the new claim of the right to exclude foreigners from trade is embodied in the Ukase of 1821.

Text of Ukase of 1821.

See Appendix, vol. I, No. 1.

The following is the translation of the Ukase which was issued by the Emperor Alexander in 1821:—

"*Edict of His Imperial Majesty, Autocrat of All the
"Russias.*

"The Directing Senate maketh known to all men: Whereas, in an Edict of His Imperial Majesty, issued to the Directing Senate on the 4th day of September [1821], and signed by His Imperial Majesty's own hand, it is thus expressed:—

"'Observing from Reports submitted to us that the trade of our subjects on the Aleutian Islands and on the north-west coast of America appertaining unto Russia is subjected, because of secret and illicit traffic, to oppression and impediments, and finding that the principal cause of these difficulties is the want of Rules establishing the boundaries for navigation along these coasts, and the order of naval communication, as well in these places as on the whole of the eastern coast of Siberia and the Kurile Islands, we have deemed it necessary to determine these communications by specific Regulations, which are hereto attached.

"'In forwarding these Regulations to the Directing Senate, we command that the same be published for universal information, and that the proper measures be taken to carry them into execution.

(Countersigned) "'COUNT D. GURIEFF,
"'*Minister of Finances.*

"'It is therefore decreed by the Directing Senate that His Imperial Majesty's Edict be published for the information of all men, and that the same be obeyed by all whom it may concern.'

(L.S.)

[The original is signed by the Directing Senate. On the original is written in the handwriting of His Imperial Majesty, thus:] Be it accord.. .XANDER.

"*Rules established for the Limits of Navigation and Order of Communication along the Coast of the Eastern Siberia, the North-west coast of America, and the Aleutian, Kurile, and other Islands.*

"'Section 1. The pursuits of commerce, whaling, and fishery, and of all other industry, on all islands, ports, and gulfs, including the whole of the north-west coast of America, beginning from Behring Straits to the 51st of northern latitude; also from the Aleutian Islands to the eastern coast of Siberia, as well as along the Kurile Islands, from Behring Straits to the south cape of the Island of Urup, viz., to the 45° 50' northern latitude, is exclusively granted to Russian subjects.

"'Section 2. It is therefore prohibited to all foreign vessels not only to land on the coasts and islands belonging to Russia, as stated above, but also to approach them within less than 100 Italian miles. The transgressor's vessel is subject to confiscation, along with the whole cargo.'"

See Appendix, vol. I, No. 1.

* * * *

By this Ukase Russia first attempted to assert, as against other nations, exclusive jurisdiction of rights over the shores of America and Asia bounding the Pacific Ocean, certain Islands therein, and over a portion of the Pacific Ocean including what is now known as Behring Sea.

The purpose of the Ukase so far as the attempted exclusion of foreigners from 100 miles of the coasts is concerned, is explained by Baron de Nicolay in his note to Lord Londonderry, the 31st October (12th November), 1821.

Ukase of 1821.

First assertion of exclusive jurisd

Purpose of Ukase of 1821.

Baron Nicolay to Lord Londonderry, October 31 (November 12), 1821.
See Appendix, vol. II, Part I, No. 1.

To prevent illicit traffic.

He insists that the operations of "smugglers" and "adventurers" on the coast—

"Have for their object not only a fraudulent commerce in furs and other articles which are exclusively reserved to the Russian-American Company, but it appears that they often betray a hostile tendency.

"It was," he continues, "therefore necessary to take severe measures against these intrigues, and to protect the Company against the considerable injury that resulted, and *it was with that end in view* that the annexed Regulation has been published."

And again—

"The Government, however, limited itself, as can be seen by the newly-published Regulation, to forbidding all foreign vessels not only to land on the Settlements of the American Company and on the peninsula of Kamtchatka and the coasts of the Okhotsk Sea, but also to sail along the coast of these possessions, and, as a rule, to approach them within 100 Italian miles."

The justification for the Ukase and the Regulations made thereunder, is stated on the face of the Ukase in the words:—

"And finding that the principal cause of these difficulties [*i.e.*, impediments caused by 'secret and illicit trafic'] is want of Rules establishing the boundaries for navigation along these coasts, * * * *."

To extend territorial jurisdiction.

That the object of the Ukase was to extend *territorial* jurisdiction over the north-west coast and islands and to prohibit the trade of foreigners, rather than to protect any existing or prospective fishery is further indicated by No. 70 of the Regulations of the Russian-American Company. This Regulation reads:—

See Appendix, vol. i, No. 2.

"70. A ship of war, after visiting, not only the Company's Settlements, but also, and more particularly, the channels which foreign merchant-vessels are likely to *frequent for the purpose of illicit trading with the natives*, will return to winter wherever the Government orders it."

Poletica to Adams, February 28, 1822. See Appendix, vol. ii, Part II, No. 1.

The motive and purpose of this Ukase is further explained by the letter of M. de Poletica, Russian Minister at Washington, dated the 28th February, 1822.

That Russia's aim was to acquire a vast North American Territory appears by the construction put by M. de Poletica on the Ukase of the Emperor Paul in 1799, as conveying to the Russian-American Company the grant of a terri-

[248]   G

torial concession down to the 55th degree of latitude, and by its justification of its further extension to the 51st degree on the American coast.

He proceeds to defend the policy of exclusion contained in the Ukase of 1821 by explaining that, as Russian possessions extend from Behring Strait to the 51st degree north latitude on the north-west coast of America, and on the opposite coast of Asia and the islands adjacent, to the 45th degree, the sea within those limits (viz., that part of the Pacific Ocean) was a close sea, over which Russia might exercise exclusive jurisdiction; but he goes on to say that Russia preferred asserting only her essential right without "taking any advantage of localities," and on these grounds the limit of 100 Italian miles is justified.

The measure he declares to be directed:—

"Against the culpable enterprises of foreign adventurers, who, not content with exercising upon the coasts above mentioned an illicit trade, very prejudicial to the rights reserved entirely to the Russian-American Company, take upon them besides to furnish arms and ammunition to the natives in the Russian possessions in America, inciting them likewise in every manner to resist and revolt against the authorities there established."

The same view is expressed in the Confidential Memorandum inclosed in the Duke of Wellington's letter to Mr. G. Canning of the 28th November, 1822. *See* p. 42.

Upon receiving communication of the Ukase, the British and United States' Governments immediately objected both to the extension of the territorial claim and to the assertion of maritime jurisdiction.

Protest of Great Britain.

The Ukase was brought to the notice of Lord Londonderry, Secretary of State for Foreign Affairs for Great Britain, in the letter already quoted of the 12th November, 1821, by Baron de Nicolay, then Russian Chargé d'Affaires as connected with the territorial rights of the Russian Crown on the north-west coast of America, and with the commerce and navigation of the Emperor's subjects in the seas adjacent thereto.

On the 18th January, 1822, four months after the issue of the Ukase, Lord Londonderry wrote

The protest of the British Government.

See Appendix, vol. II, Part I, No. 1.

Correspondence between Great Britain and Russia.

See Appendix, vol. ii, Part I, No. 7.

in the following terms to Count Lieven, the Russian Ambassador in London:—

"In the meantime, upon the subject of this Ukase generally, and especially upon the two main principles of claim laid down therein, viz., an *exclusive sovereignty* alleged to belong to Russia over the territories therein described, as also the *exclusive right of navigating and trading within the maritime limits therein set forth*, His Britannic Majesty must be understood as *hereby reserving all his rights*, not being prepared to admit that the intercourse which is allowed on the face of this instrument to have hitherto subsisted on those coasts and in those seas can be deemed to be illicit, or *that the ships of friendly Powers*, even supposing an unqualified sovereignty was proved to appertain to the Imperial Crown in those vast and very imperfectly occupied territories, *could, by the acknowledged law of nations be excluded from navigating within the distance of* 100 *Italian miles, as therein laid down from the coast*, the exclusive dominion of which is assumed (but as His Majesty's Government conceive in error) to belong to His Imperial Majesty the Emperor of All the Russias."

Ibid., vol. ii, Part I, No. 14.

The Duke of Wellington having been appointed British Plenipotentiary at the Congress of Verona, Mr. G. Canning, then Secretary of State for Foreign Affairs, addressed to him, on the 27th September, 1822, a despatch in which he dealt with the claim in the Ukase for the extension of territorial rights over adjacent seas to the distance —" unprecedented distance," he terms it—of 100 miles from the coast, and of closing "a hitherto unobstructed passage."

In this despatch Mr. Canning says:—

Abandonment of claim to extraordinary jurisdiction.

"I have, indeed, the satisfaction to believe, from a conference which I have had with Count Lieven on this matter, that upon these two points,—the attempt to shut up the passage altogether, and the claim of exclusive dominion to so enormous a distance from the coast,— the Russian Government are prepared entirely to waive their pretensions. The only effort that has been made to justify the latter claim was by reference to an Article in the Treaty of Utrecht, which assigns 30 leagues from the coast as the distance of prohibition. But to this argument it is sufficient to answer, that the assumption of such a space was, in the instance quoted, by stipulation in a Treaty, and one to which, therefore, the party to be affected by it had (whether wisely or not) given its deliberate consent. No inference could be drawn from that transaction in favour of a claim by authority against all the world.

"I have little doubt, therefore, but that the public notification of the claim to consider the portions of the ocean included between the adjoining coasts of America and the

Russian Empire as a *mare clausum*, and to extend the exclusive territorial jurisdiction of Russia to 100 Italian miles from the coast, will be publicly recalled, and I have the King's commands to instruct your Grace further to require of the Russian Minister (on the ground of the facts and reasonings furnished in their (sic) despatch and its inclosures) that such a portion of territory alone shall be defined as belonging to Russia as shall not interfere with the rights and actual possessions of His Majesty's subjects in North America."

On the 17th October in the same year, the Duke of Wellington, at Verona, addressed to Count Nesselrode, the Russian Plenipotentiary at the Congress, a Confidential Memorandum containing the following words:—

"Objecting, as we do, to this claim of exclusive sovereignty on the part of Russia, I might save myself the trouble of discussing the particular mode of its exercise as set forth in this Ukase, but we object to the mode in which the sovereignty is proposed to be exercised under this Ukase, not less than we do to the claim of it. *We cannot admit the right of any Power possessing the sovereignty of a country to exclude the vessels of others from the seas on its coasts to the distance of 100 Italian miles.*"

[margin: Confidential Memorandum inclosed in letter of Duke of Wellington to G. Canning, November 28, 1822. See Appendix, vol. ii, Part I, No. 1⁵.]

In reply, Count Nesselrode communicated to the Duke of Wellington a "Confidential Memorandum" dated the 11th (23rd) November, 1822, which contains the following passages:—

[margin: Ibid.]

"The Cabinet of Russia has taken into mature consideration the Confidential Memorandum forwarded to them by the Duke of Wellington on the 17th October last, relative to the measures adopted by His Majesty the Emperor, under date of the 4th (16th) September, 1821, for defining the extent of the Russian possessions on the north-west coast of America, and for forbidding foreign vessels to approach his possessions within a distance of 100 Italian miles.

". . . . It was on the contrary, because she regarded those rights of sovereignty as legitimate, and because imperious considerations involving the very existence of the commerce which she carries on in the regions of the north-west coast of America compelled her to establish a system of precautions which became indispensable that she caused the Ukase of the 4th (16th) September, 1821, to be issued.

". . . . Consequently, the Emperor has charged his Cabinet to declare to the Duke of Wellington (such declaration not to prejudice his rights in any way if it be not accepted) that he is ready to fix, by means of friendly negotiation, and on the basis of mutual accommodation, the degrees of latitude and longitude which the two Powers shall regard as the utmost limit of their possessions and of their establishments on the north-west coast of America.

[margin: Correspondence between Great Britain and Russia.]

Correspondence between Great Britain and Russia.

"His Imperial Majesty is pleased to believe that this negotiation can be completed without difficulty to the mutual satisfaction of the two States; and the Cabinet of Russia can from this moment assure the Duke of Wellington that the measures of precaution and supervision which will then be taken on the Russian part of the coast of America will be entirely in conformity with the rights derived from sovereignty, and with the established customs of nations, and that there will be no possibility of legitimate cause of complaint against them."

Again, on the 28th November, 1822, the Duke of Wellington addressed a note to Count Lieven, containing the following words:—

See Appendix, vol. ii, Part I, No. 15.

"The second ground on which we object to the Ukase is that His Imperial Majesty thereby excludes from a certain considerable extent of the open sea vessels of other nations. We contend that the assumption of this power is contrary to the law of nations, and we cannot found a negotiation upon a paper in which it is again broadly asserted. We contend that no Power whatever can exclude another from the use of the open sea. A Power can exclude itself from the navigation of a certain coast, sea, &c., by its own act or engagement, but it cannot by right be excluded by another. This we consider as the law of nations, and we cannot negotiate upon a paper in which a right is asserted inconsistent with this principle."

At an early date in the course of the negotiations with the United States and with Great Britain the execution of the Ukase beyond the territorial limit of 3 miles was suspended. Indeed, as far as the waters of Behring Sea are concerned, it may safely be said that it was never put into practical execution beyond this limit. The note from Count Nesselrode to Mr. Middleton on the subject was dated the 1st August, 1822, and is thus alluded to by Mr. Middleton in a despatch to Mr. Adams of the 19th September, 1823:—

See Apendix, vol ii, Part I, No. 31.

American State Papers, Foreign Relations, vol. v, p. 448.

"Upon Sir Charles [Bagot] expressing his wish to be informed respecting the actual state of the *north-west* question between the United States and Russia, so far as it might be known to me, I saw no objection to making a *confidential* communication to him of the note of Count Nesselrode, dated the 1st August, 1822, by which, in fact, staying the execution of the Ukase above mentioned, Russia has virtually abandoned the pretensions therein advanced.

See Appendix, vol. ii, Part I, No. 20.

The communication to the British Government on the same subject was made in August 1823 in the shape of an extract from a despatch from Count Nesselrode to Count Lieven, dated the 20th June, 1823. The following passage in it shows how complete was the abandonment of the unusual claim of maritime jurisdiction:—

Correspondence between Great Britain and Russia.

Abandonment of claim to extraordinary jurisdiction.

"That the Commanders of our ships of war must confine their surveillance as nearly as possible to the mainland, *i.e.*, over an extent of sea within range of cannon-shot from the shore; that they must not extend that surveillance beyond the sphere where the American Company has effectually exercised its rights of hunting and fishing since the date of its creation, as well as since the renewal of its privileges in 1799, and that, as to the islands on which are to be found colonies or settlements of the Company, they are all indistinctively comprised in this general rule.

". . . . . Your Excellency will observe that these new instructions—which, as a matter of fact, are to suspend provisionally the effect of the Imperial Ukase of the 4th September, 1821—were sent from St. Petersburgh only in August of last year."

Mr. Lyall, Chairman of the Ship-owners' Society, of London, wrote on the 19th November, 1823, to Mr. G. Canning, asking whether official advices had been received from St. Peterburg that the Ukase of 1821 had been annulled. Mr. Canning having privately submitted his proposed reply to Count Lieven for his comments, caused the following letter to be sent, which had received Count Lieven's approval:—

See Appendix, vol. ii, Part I, Nos. 33, 34, and 35.

"I am directed by Mr. Secretary Canning to acknowledge the receipt of your letter of the 19th instant, expressing a hope that the Ukase of September 1821 had been annulled.

Lord F. Conyngham to Mr. Lyall, November 26, 1823. See Appendix, vol. ii, Part I, No. 36.

"Mr. Canning cannot authorize me to state to you in distinct terms that the Ukase has been '*annulled*,' because the negotiation to which it gave rise is still pending, embracing, as it does, many points of great intricacy as well as importance.

"But I am directed by Mr. Canning to acquaint you that orders have been sent out by the Court of St. Petersburg to their Naval Commanders calculated to prevent any collision between Russian ships and those of other nations, and, in effect, suspending the Ukase of September 1821."

On the 15th January, 1824, Mr. G. Canning wrote to Sir C. Bagot, the British Ambassador at St. Petersburg:—

See Appendix, vol. ii, Part I, No. 37.

". . . . . The questions at issue between Great Britain and Russia are short and simple. The Russian Ukase contains two objectionable pretensions: First, an extravagant assumption of maritime supremacy; secondly, an unwarranted claim of territorial dominions.

Correspondence between Great Britain and Russia.

Abandonment of claim to extraordinary jurisdiction.

"As to the first, the disavowal of Russia is, in substance all that we could desire. Nothing remains for negotiation on that head but to clothe that disavowal in precise and satisfactory terms. We would much rather that those terms should be suggested by Russia herself than have the air of pretending to dictate them; you will therefore request Count Nesselrode to furnish you with his notion of such a declaration on this point as may be satisfactory to your Government. That declaration may be made the preamble of the convention of limits." . . . .

Again, in a despatch, 24th July, 1824, to Sir C. Bagot, Mr. G. Canning says:—

See Appendix, vol. ii, Part I, No. 44.

" . . . . Your Excellency will observe that there are but two points which have struck Count Lieven as susceptible of any question. The first, the assumption of the base of the mountains, instead of the summit as the line of boundary; the second, the extension of the right of the navigation of the Pacific to the sea beyond Behring Straits.

* * * *

"As to the second point, it is, perhaps, as Count Lieven remarks, new. But it is to be remarked, in return, that the circumstances under which this additional security is required will be new also.

"By the territorial demarcation agreed to in this 'projet,' Russia will become possessed, in acknowledged sovereignty of both sides, of Behring Straits.

"The Power which could think of making the Pacific a *mare clausum* may not unnaturally be supposed capable of a disposition to apply the same character to a strait comprehended between two shores of which it becomes the undisputed owner; but the shutting up of Behring Straits, or the power to shut them up hereafter, would be a thing not to be tolerated by England.

See *ante*, p. 32.

"Nor could we submit to be excluded, either positively or constructively, from a sea in which the skill and science of our seamen has been and is still employed in enterprises interesting not to this country alone, but to the whole civilized world.

"The protection given by the Convention to the American coasts of each Power may (if it is thought necessary) be extended in terms to the coasts of the Russian Asiatic territory; but in some way or other, if not in the form now prescribed, the free navigation of Behring Straits and of the seas beyond them must be secured to us."

See Appendix, vol. ii, Part I, No. 52.

Mr. George Canning in a despatch to Mr. Stratford Canning, who had been appointed British Plenipotentiary for the negotiation of a Convention at St. Petersburg, under date the 8th December, 1824, after giving a summary of the negotiations up to that date, goes on to say:—

"It is comparatively indifferent to us whether we hasten or postpone all questions respecting the limits of territorial possession on the continent of America, but the pretensions of the Russian Ukase of 1821 to exclusive dominion over the Pacific could not continue longer unrepealed without compelling us to take some measure of public and effectual remonstrance against it.

"You will therefore take care, in the first instance, to repress any attempt to give this change to the character of the negotiation, and will declare without reserve that the point to which alone the solicitude of the British Government and the jealousy of the British nation attach any great importance is the doing away (in a manner as little disagreeable to Russia as possible) of the effect of the Ukase of 1821.

"That this Ukase is not acted upon, and that instructions have been long ago sent by the Russian Government to their cruizers in the Pacific to suspend the execution of its provisions, is true; but a private disavowal of a published claim is no security against the revival of that claim. The suspension of the execution of a principle may be perfectly compatible with the continued maintenance of the principle itself, and when we have seen in the course of this negotiation that the Russian claim to the possession of the coast of America down to latitude 59° [sic] rests in fact on no other ground than the presumed acquiescence of the nations of Europe in the provisions of an Ukase published by the Emperor Paul in the year 1799, against which it is affirmed that no public remonstrance was made, it becomes us to be exceedingly careful that we do not, by a similar neglect, on the present occasion allow a similar presumption to be raised as to an acquiescence in the Ukase of 1821.

"The right of the subjects of His Majesty to navigate freely in the Pacific cannot be held as a matter of indulgence from any Power. Having once been publicly questioned, it must be publicly acknowledged.

"We do not desire that any distinct reference should be made to the Ukase of 1821; but we do feel it necessary that the statement of our right should be clear and positive, and that it should stand forth in the Convention in the place which properly belongs to it, as a plain and substantive stipulation, and not be brought in as an incidental consequence of other arrangements to which we attach comparatively little importance.

"This stipulation stands in the front of the Convention concluded between Russia and the United States of America; and we see no reason why upon similar claims we should not obtain exactly the like satisfaction.

"For reasons of the same nature we cannot consent that the liberty of navigation through Bering Straits should be stated in the Treaty as a boon from Russia.

"The tendency of such a statement would be to give countenance to those claims of exclusive jurisdiction against which we, on our own behalf, and on that of the whole civilized world, protest.

* * * *"

Correspondence between Great Britain and Russia.

Abandonment of claim to extraordinary jurisdiction.

See *post*, p. 5?.

Correspondence between Great Britain and Russia.

Abandonment of claim to extraordinary jurisdiction.

"It will of course strike the Russian Plenipotentiaries that, by the adoption of the American Article respecting navigation, &c., the provision for an exclusive fishery of 2 leagues from the coasts of our respective possessions falls to the ground.

"But the omission is, in truth, immaterial.

"The law of nations assigns the exclusive sovereignty of 1 league to each Power on its own coasts, without any specific stipulation, and though Sir Charles Bagot was authorized to sign the Convention with the specific stipulation of 2 leagues, in ignorance of what had been decided in the American Convention at the time, yet, after that Convention has been some months before the world, and after the opportunity of consideration has been forced upon us by the act of Russia herself, we cannot now consent, in negotiating *de novo*, to a stipulation which, while it is absolutely unimportant to any practical good, would appear to establish a contrast between the United States and us to our disadvantage."

The Treaty (Great Britain and Russia) February 28, 1825.

These negotiations resulted in a Convention with Great Britain, signed on the 28th February, 1825, hereinafter referred to.

Protest of United States against Ukase of 1821.

Protest of the United States.

50th Cong., 2nd Sess., Sen. Ex. Doc. No. 106, p. 204.

On the 30th January (11th February), 1822, M. Pierre de Poletica, the Envoy Extraordinary and Minister Plenipotentiary of the Russian Emperor, transmitted the Ukase to Mr. Adams, Secretary of State for the United States.

Ibid., p. 205.

On the 25th February, 1822, Mr. Adams wrote to M. Poletica:—

"*Department of State, Washington,*
"Sir,   *February* 25, 1822.

"I have the honour of receiving your note of the 11th instant, inclosing a printed copy of the Regulations adopted by the Russian-American Company, and sanctioned by His Imperial Majesty, relating to the commerce of foreigners in the waters bordering on the establishments of that Company upon the north-west coast of America.

"I am directed by the President of the United States to inform you that he has seen with surprise, in this Edict, the assertion of a territorial claim on the part of Russia, extending to the 51st degree of north latitude on this continent, and a Regulation interdicting to all commercial vessels other than Russian, upon the penalty of seizure and confiscation, the approach upon the high seas within 100 Italian miles of the shores to which that claim is made to apply. The relations of the United States with His Imperial Majesty have always been of the most friendly character; and it is the earnest desire of this Government to preserve them in that state. It was expected, before any Act which should define the boundary

[248]   H

between the territories of the United States and Russia on this continent, that the same would have been arranged by Treaty between the parties. To exclude the vessels of our citizens from the shore, beyond the ordinary distance to which the territorial jurisdiction extends, has excited still greater surprise.

"This Ordinance affects so deeply the rights of the United States and of their citizens, that I am instructed to inquire whether you are authorized to give explanations of the grounds of right, upon principles generally recognized by the laws and usages of nations, which can warrant the claims and Regulations contained in it.

"I avail, &c.
(Signed) "JOHN QUINCY ADAMS."

It will be observed that both the Ukase and the protest apply to the waters from Behring Strait southward as far as the 51st degree of latitude on the coast of America.

On the 28th of the same month the Russian Representative replied at length, defending the territorial claim on grounds of discovery, first occupation, and undisturbed possession, and explaining the motive which determined the Imperial Government in framing the Ukase.

He wrote:—

"I shall be more succinct, Sir, in the exposition of the motives which determined the Imperial Government to prohibit foreign vessels from approaching the north-west coast of America belonging to Russia within the distance of at least 100 Italian miles. This measure, however severe it may at first appear, is, after all, but a measure of prevention. It is exclusively directed against the culpable enterprises of foreign adventurers, who, not content with exercising upon the coasts above mentioned an illicit trade very prejudicial to the rights reserved entirely to the Russian-American Company, take upon them besides to furnish arms and ammunition to the natives in the Russian possessions in America, exciting them likewise in every manner to resist and revolt against the authorities there established.

"The American Government doubtless recollects that the irregular conduct of these adventurers, the majority of whom was composed of American citizens, has been the object of the most pressing remonstrances on the part of Russia to the Federal Government from the time that Diplomatic Missions were organized between the countries. These remonstrances, repeated at different times, remain constantly without effect, and the inconveniences to which they ought to bring a remedy continue to increase. . . . .

"I ought, in the last place, to request you to consider, Sir, that the Russian possessions in the Pacific Ocean extend, on the north-west coast of America, from Behring Strait to the 51st degree of north latitude, and on the opposite side of Asia and the islands adjacent, from the

Protest of United States against Ukase of 1821.

Russian Defence of Ukase.

M. de Poletica to Mr. J. Q. Adams, February 28, 1822, American State Papers, Foreign Relations, vol. iv, pp. 861–862. See Appendix, vol. ii, Part II, No 1.

Ukase based on doctrine of mare clausum.

same strait to the 45th degree. The extent of sea of which these possessions form the limits comprehends all the conditions which are ordinarily attached to *shut seas* ("mers fermées"), and the Russian Government might consequently judge itself authorized to exercise upon this sea the right of sovereignty, and especially that of entirely interdicting the entrance of foreigners. But it preferred only asserting its essential rights, without taking any advantage of localities."

<small>ice between United States and Russia.</small>

<small>50th Cong., 2nd Sess., Senate Ex. Doc. No. 106, p. 207. See Appendix, vol. ii, Part II, No 2.</small>

To this Mr. Adams replied (30th March, 1822). He said:—

"This pretension is to be considered not only with reference to the question of territorial right, but also to that prohibition to the vessels of other nations, including those of the United States, to approach within 100 Italian miles of the coasts. From the period of the existence of the United States, as an independent nation, their vessels have freely navigated those seas, and the right to navigate them is a part of that independence.

"With regard to the suggestion that the Russian Government might have justified the exercise of sovereignty over the Pacific Ocean as a close sea, because it claims territory both on its American and Asiatic shores, it may suffice to say that the distance from shore to shore on this sea, in latitude 51° north, is not less than 90° of longitude, or 4,000 miles."

The Russian Representative replied to this note on the 2nd April following, and in the course of his letter he said:—

<small>M. de Poletica to Mr. J. Q. Adams, April 2, 1822. 50th Cong., 2nd Sess., Senate Ex. Doc. No. 106, p. 208.</small>

"In the same manner the great extent of the Pacific Ocean at the 51st degree of latitude can not invalidate the right which Russia may have of considering that part of the ocean as close. But as the Imperial Government has not thought fit to take advantage of that right, all further discussion on this subject would be idle.

"As to the right claimed for the citizens of the United States of trading with the natives of the country of the north-west coast of America, without the limits of the jurisdiction belonging to Russia, the Imperial Government will not certainly think of limiting it, and still less of attacking it there. But I cannot dissemble, Sir, that this same trade beyond the 51st degree will meet with difficulties and inconveniences, for which the American owners will only have to accuse their own imprudence after the publicity which has been given to the measures taken by the Imperial Government for maintaining the rights of the Russian-American Company in their absolute integrity.

"I shall not finish this letter without repeating to you, Sir, the very positive assurance which I have already had the honour once of expressing to you that in every case where the American Government shall judge it necessary to make explanations to that of the Emperor, the President of the United States may rest assured that these explanations will always be attended to by the Emperor, my august Sovereign, with the most friendly, and, consequently, the most conciliatory, dispositions."

Correspondence between United States and Russia.

On the 22nd July, 1823, Mr. Adams wrote to Mr. Middleton, the United States' Minister at St. Petersburg, as follows:—

"From the tenour of the Ukase, the pretensions of the Imperial Government extend to an exclusive territorial jurisdiction from the 45th degree of north latitude, on the Asiatic coast, to the latitude of 51 north on the western coast of the American Continent; and they assume the right of interdicting the navigation and the fishery of all other nations to the extent of 100 miles from the whole of that coast.

50th Cong., 2nd Sess., Senate Ex. Doc. No. 106, p. 210. See Appendix, vol. ii, Part II, No. 3.

"The United States can admit no part of these claims. Their right of navigation and of fishing is perfect, and has been in constant exercise from the earliest times, after the Peace of 1783, throughout the whole extent of the Southern Ocean, subject only to the ordinary exceptions and exclusions of the territorial jurisdictions, which, so far as Russian rights are concerned, are confined to certain islands north of the 55th degree of latitude, and have no existence on the Continent of America.

"The correspondence between M. Poletica and this Department contained no discussion of the principles or of the facts upon which he attempted the justification of the Imperial Ukase. This was purposely avoided on our part, under the expectation that the Imperial Government could not fail, upon a review of the measure, to revoke it altogether. It did, however, excite much public animadversion in this country, as the Ukase itself had already done in England. I inclose herewith the North American Review for October 1822, No. 37, which contains an article (p. 370) written by a person fully master of the subject; and for the view of it taken in England I refer you to the 52nd number of the Quarterly Review, the article upon Lieutenant Kotzebue's voyages. From the article in the North American Review it will be seen that the rights of discovery, of occupancy, and of uncontested possession, alleged by M. Poletica, are all without foundation in fact."

* * * *

Mr. Middleton, writing to the Secretary of State of the United States, on the 1st December, 1823, inclosed a confidential memorial which thus dealt with the claim (which is properly regarded by him as an attempt to extend territorial jurisdiction upon the theory of a shut sea and having no other basis):—

"The extension of territorial rights to the distance of 100 miles from the coasts upon two opposite continents,

American State Papers, Foreign Relations, vol. v, p. 462.

51

Correspondence between United States and Russia.

See Appendix,
vol. ii, Part II,
No. 5.

and the prohibition of approaching to the same distance from these coasts, or from those of all the intervening islands, are innovations in the law of nations, and measures unexampled. It must thus be imagined that this prohibition, bearing the pains of confiscation, applies to a long line of coasts, with the intermediate islands, situated in vast seas, where the navigation is subject to innumerable and unknown difficulties, and where the chief employment, which is the whale fishery, cannot be compatible with a regulated and well-determined course.

"The right cannot be denied of shutting a port, a sea, or even an entire country, against foreign commerce in some particular cases. But the exercise of such a right, unless in the case of a colonial system already established, or for some other special object, would be exposed to an unfavourable interpretation, as being contrary to the liberal spirit of modern times, wherein we look for the bonds of amity and of reciprocal commerce among all nations being more closely cemented.

"Universal usage, which has obtained the force of law, has established for all the coasts an accessory limit of a moderate distance, which is sufficient for the security of the country and for the convenience of its inhabitants, but which lays no restraint upon the universal rights of nations, nor upon the freedom of commerce and of navigation." (Vattel, Book 1, Chapter 23, section 289.)

American State Papers, Foreign Relations, vol. v, pp. 465, 466.

At the fourth Conference (8th March, 1824) which preceded the signature of the Treaty of the 5th (17th) April, 1824, Mr. Middleton, the United States' Representative, submitted to Count Nesselrode the following paper:—

"(Translation.)

"The dominion cannot be acquired but by a real occupation and possession, and an intention ('animus') to establish it is by no means sufficient.

"Now, it is clear, according to the facts established, that neither Russia nor any other European Power has the right of dominion upon the Continent of America between the 50th and 60th degrees of north latitude.

"Still less has she the dominion of the adjacent maritime territory, or of the sea which washes these coasts, a dominion which is only accessory to the territorial dominion.

"Therefore she has not the right of exclusion or of admission on these coasts, nor in these seas, which are free seas.

"The right of navigating all the free seas belongs, by natural law, to every independent nation, and even constitutes an essential part of this independence.

"The United States have exercised navigation in the seas, and commerce upon the coasts above mentioned, from the time of their independence: and they have a perfect right to this navigation and to this commerce, and they can only be deprived of it by their own act or by a Convention."

Convention between the United States and Russia.

The result of these negotiations between the United States and Russia was the Convention of the 17th April, 1824, which put an end to any further pretension on the part of Russia to restrict navigation or fishing in Behring Sea, so far as citizens of the United States were concerned.

The English version of the Convention is as follows:—

The Treaty (Russia and the United States), April 17, 1824.

For French text, see Appendix, vol. ii, Part III, No. 1.

Blue Book, "United States No. 1 (1891)," p. 57. Appendix, vol. iii. Navigation of Pacific to be free.

"ARTICLE I.

"It is agreed that in any part of the Great Ocean, commonly called the Pacific Ocean, or South Sea, the respective citizens or subjects of the High Contracting Powers shall be neither disturbed nor restrained, either in navigation or in fishing, or in the power of resorting to the coasts, upon points which may not already have been occupied, for the purpose of trading with the natives, saving always the restrictions and conditions determined by the following Articles.

"ARTICLE II.

"With a view of preventing the rights of navigation and of fishing, exercised upon the Great Ocean by the citizens and subjects of the High Contracting Powers, from becoming the pretext for an illicit trade, it is agreed that the citizens of the United States shall not resort to any point where there is a Russian Establishment, without the permission of the Governor or Commander; and that, reciprocally, the subjects of Russia shall not resort, without permission, to any Establishment of the United States upon the north-west coast.

"ARTICLE III.

"It is, moreover, agreed that hereafter there shall not be formed by the citizens of the United States, or under the authority of the said States, any Establishment upon the north-west coast of America, nor in any of the islands adjacent, to the north of 54° 40' of north latitude; and that, in the same manner there shall be none formed by Russian subjects, or under the authority of Russia, south of the same parallel.

"ARTICLE IV.

"It is, nevertheless, understood that, during a term of ten years, counting from the signature of the present Convention, the ships of both Powers, or which belong to their citizens or subjects respectively, may reciprocally frequent, without any hindrance whatever, the interior seas, gulfs, harbours, and creeks upon the coast mentioned in the preceding Article, for the purpose of fishing and trading with the natives of the country.

"ARTICLE V.

Treaty of 1824.

"All spirituous liquors, fire-arms, other arms, powder, and munitions of war of every kind are always excepted from this same commerce permitted by the preceding Article; and the two Powers engage reciprocally neither to sell, or suffer them to be sold to the natives, by their respective citizens and subjects, nor by any person who may be under their authority. It is likewise stipulated that this restriction shall never afford a pretext, nor be advanced, in any case, to authorize either search or detention of the vessels, seizure of the merchandize, or, in fine, any measures of constraint whatever towards the merchants or the crews who may carry on this commerce; the High Contracting Powers reciprocally reserving to themselves to determine upon the penalties to be incurred, and to inflict the punishments in case of the contravention of this Article, by their respective citizens or subjects.

"ARTICLE VI.

"When this Convention shall have been duly ratified by the President of the United States, with the advice and consent of the Senate on the one part, and on the other, by His Majesty the Emperor of all the Russias, the ratifications shall be exchanged at Washington in the space of ten months from the date below, or sooner if possible.

"In faith whereof the respective Plenipotentiaries have signed this Convention, and thereto affixed the seals of their arms.

"Done at St. Petersburg the 5th (17th) April in the year of Grace 1824.

(L.S.) "HENRY MIDDLETON.
(L.S.) "LE COMTE C. DE NESSELRODE.
(L.S.) "PIERRE DE POLETICA."

Convention between Great Britain and Russia.

(Great Britain and Russia), February 28, 1825.

The negotiations between Great Britain and Russia resulted in the Convention of the 28th February, 1825.

For French text, see Appendix, vol. II, Part I'I, No. 2.

The following is the English translation of this Convention :—

"ARTICLE I.

gation of Pacific to be free.

See Blue Book, "United States No. 1 (1891)." p. 58. Appendix, vol. iii.

"It is agreed that the respective subjects of the High Contracting Parties shall not be troubled or molested in any part of the ocean, commonly called the Pacific Ocean, either in navigating the same, in fishing therein, or in landing at such parts of the coast as shall not have been already occupied, in order to trade with the natives, under the restrictions and conditions specified in the following Articles.

"ARTICLE II.

"In order to prevent the right of navigating and fishing exercised upon the ocean by the subjects of the High Contracting Parties, from becoming the pretext for an illicit commerce, it is agreed that the subjects of His Britannic Majesty shall not land at any place where there may be a Russian establishment without the permission of the Governor or Commandant; and, on the other hand, that Russian subjects shall not land without permission at any British establishment on the north-west coast.

Treaty of 1825

"ARTICLE III.

"The line of demarcation between the possessions of the High Contracting Parties upon the coast of the continent and the islands of America to the north-west, shall be drawn in the manner following:—

"Commencing from the southernmost part of the island called Prince of Wales' Island, which point lies in the parallel of 54° 40' north latitude, and between the 131st and the 133rd degree of west longitude (meridian of Greenwich), the said line shall ascend to the north along the channel called Portland Channel, as far as the point of the continent, where it strikes the 56th degree of north latitude; from this last-mentioned point, the line of demarcation shall follow the summit of the mountains situated parallel to the coast, as far as the point of intersection of the 141st degree of west longitude (of the same meridian); and, finally, from the said point of intersection, the said meridian-line of the 141st degree, in its prolongation as far as the Frozen Ocean, shall form the limit between the Russian and British possessions on the continent of America to the north-west.

"ARTICLE IV.

"With reference to the line of demarcation laid down in the preceding Article, it is understood:

"1st. That the island called Prince of Wales' Island shall belong wholly to Russia.

"2nd. That wherever the summit of the mountains which extend in a direction parallel to the coast, from the 56th degree of north latitude to the point of intersection of the 141st degree of west longitude, shall prove to be at the distance of more than 10 marine leagues from the ocean, the limit between the British possessions and the line of coast which is to belong to Russia, as above mentioned, shall be formed by a line parallel to the windings of the coast, and which shall never exceed the distance of 10 marine leagues therefrom.

"ARTICLE V.

"It is moreover agreed that no establishment shall be formed by either of the two parties within the limits assigned by the two preceding Articles to the possessions of the other; consequently British subjects shall not

Treaty of 1825.

form any establishment either upon the coast or upon the border of the continent comprised within the limits of the Russian possessions, as designated in the two preceding Articles; and, in like manner, no establishment shall be formed by Russian subjects beyond the said limits.

"ARTICLE VI.

"It is understood that the subjects of His Britannic Majesty, from whatever quarter they may arrive, whether from the ocean or from the interior of the continent, shall for ever enjoy the right of navigating freely, and without any hindrance whatever, all the rivers and streams which, in their course towards the Pacific Ocean, may cross the line of demarcation upon the line of coast described in Article III of the present Convention.

"ARTICLE VII.

"It is also understood that, for the space of ten years from the signature of the present Convention, the vessels of the two Powers, or those belonging to their respective subjects, shall mutually be at liberty to frequent, without any hindrance whatever, all the inland seas, the gulfs, havens, and creeks on the coast mentioned in Article III, for the purposes of fishing and of trading with the natives.

"ARTICLE VIII.

"The port of Sitka, or Novo Archangelsk, shall be open to the commerce and vessels of British subjects for the space of ten years from the date of the exchange of the ratifications of the present Convention. In the event of an extension of this term of ten years being granted to any other Power, the like extension shall be granted also to Great Britain.

"ARTICLE IX.

"The above-mentioned liberty of commerce shall not apply to the trade in spirituous liquors, in fire-arms, or other arms, gunpowder, or other warlike stores; the High Contracting Parties reciprocally engaging not to permit the above-mentioned articles to be sold or delivered, in any manner whatever, to the natives of the country.

"ARTICLE X.

"Every British or Russian vessel navigating the Pacific Ocean which may be compelled by storms or by accident to take shelter in the ports of the respective Parties, shall be at liberty to refit therein, to provide itself with all necessary stores, and to put to sea again, without paying any other than port and lighthouse dues, which shall be the same as those paid by national vessels. In case, however, the master of such vessel should be under the necessity of disposing of a part of his merchandize in order to defray his expenses, he shall conform himself to the Regulations and Tariffs of the place where he may have landed.

[24S]   I

"ARTICLE XI.

"In every case of complaint on account of an infraction of the Articles of the present Convention, the civil and military authorities of the High Contracting Parties, without previously acting or taking any forcible measure, shall make an exact and circumstantial report of the matter to their respective Courts, who engage to settle the same in a friendly manner, and according to the principles of justice.

"ARTICLE XII.

"The present Convention shall be ratified, and the ratifications shall be exchanged at London within the space of six weeks, or sooner if possible.

"In witness whereof the respective Plenipotentiaries have signed the same, and have affixed thereto the seal of their arms.

"Done at St. Petersburgh the 16th (28th) day of February, in the year of our Lord one thousand eight hundred and twenty-five.

(L.S.) "STRATFORD CANNING.
(L.S.) "The Count DE NESSELRODE.
(L.S.) "PIERRE DE POLETICA."

Treaty of 1825.

Mr. Stratford Canning to Mr. G. Canning, in his despatch of the 1st March, 1825, inclosing the Convention as signed, says:—

"With respect to Behring Straits, I am happy to have it in my power to assure you, on the joint authority of the Russian Plenipotentiaries, that the Emperor of Russia has no intention whatever of maintaining any exclusive claim to the navigation of those straits, or of the seas to the north of them."

See Appendix, vol. ii, Part I, No. 56.

Mr. S. Canning, in a further despatch to Mr. G. Canning, 3rd (15th) April, 1825, said:—

". . . . With respect to the right of fishing, no explanation whatever took place between the Plenipotentiaries and myself in the course of our negotiations. As no objection was started by them to the Article which I offered in obedience to your instructions, I thought it unadvisable to raise a discussion on the question; and the distance from the coast at which the right of fishing is to be exercised in common passed without specification, and consequently rests on the law of nations as generally received.

"Conceiving, however, at a later period that you might possibly wish to declare the law of nations thereon, jointly with the Court of Russia, in some ostensible shape, I broached the matter anew to Count Nesselrode, and suggested that he should authorize Count Lieven, on your invitation, to exchange notes with you declamatory of the law as fixing the distance at 1 marine league from the shore.

Ibid., No. 57.

"Count Nesselrode replied that he should feel embarrassed in submitting this suggestion to the Emperor just at the moment when the ratifications of the Convention were on the point of being dispatched to London; and he seemed exceedingly desirous that nothing should happen to retard the accomplishment of that essential formality. He assured me at the same time that his Government would be content, in executing the Convention, to abide by the recognized law of nations; and that, if any question should hereafter be raised upon the subject, he should not refuse to join in making the suggested declaration, on being satisfied that the general rule under the law of nations was such as we supposed.

"Having no authority to press the point in question, I took the assurance thus given by Count Nesselrode as sufficient, in all probability, to answer every national purpose...."

The claim of Russia attracted much attention at the time.

States' interpretation of Russo-American Treaty.

President Monroe wrote to Mr. Madison on the 2nd August, 1824, with reference to the Convention of that year, to the effect that—

Wharton, Digest of International Law, section 159, vol. ii, p. 226.

"By this Convention the claim to the *mare clausum* is given up, a very high northern latitude is established for our boundary with Russia, and our trade with the Indians placed for ten years on a perfectly free footing, and after that term left open for negotiation.... England will, of course, have a similar stipulation in favour of the free navigation of the Pacific, but we shall have the credit of having taken the lead in the affair."

In answer to the above, Mr. Madison wrote to President Monroe on the 5th August, 1824:—

Letters and writings of James Madison. Philadelphia, 1865, p. 446.

"The Convention with Russia is a propitious event, as substituting amicable adjustment for the risk of hostile collision. But I give the Emperor, however, little credit for his assent to the principle of '*mare Liberater*' [sic] in the North Pacific. His pretensions were so absurd, and so disgusting to the maritime world, that he could not do better than retreat from them through the forms of negotiation. It is well that the cautious, if not courteous, policy of England towards Russia has had the effect of making us, in the public eye, the leading Power in arresting her expansive ambition."

The Ukase never enforced.

See Letter of S. Canning to G. Canning, April 21, 1823. Appendix, vol. ii, Part I, No. 24. See post, p. 78.

In the year 1822 the Russian authorities attempted to enforce the provisions of the Ukase of 1821 and seized the United States' brig "Pearl," when on a voyage from Boston to Sitka. The circumstances of this case are stated in the next Chapter.

It is sufficient for the present purpose to note

that the United States at once protested, the "Pearl" was released, and compensation paid for her arrest and detention.

This is believed to be the only case in which any attempt was, in practice, made by Russia to interfere with any ship of another nation in the waters in question outside of territorial limits.

The facts disclosed in this Chapter show:—

That the Ukase of the Emperor Paul in the year 1821—the first and only attempt on the part of Russia to assert dominion over, and restrict the rights of other nations in, the non-territorial waters of the North Pacific, including those of Behring Sea—was made the subject of immediate and emphatic protest by Great Britain and the United States of America.

That Russia thereupon unequivocally withdrew her claims to such exclusive dominion and right of control.

That the Conventions of 1824 and 1825 declared and recognized the rights of the subjects of Great Britain and the United States to navigate and fish in all parts of the non-territorial waters over which the Ukase purported to extend.

Chapter III.

Head (C).—*The question whether the body of water now known as the Behring Sea is included in the phrase "Pacific Ocean," as used in the Treaty of 1825 between Great Britain and Russia.*

"Pacific Ocean" as used in the Treaty of 1825.

It will be remembered that the Ukase of 1821 included the Pacific from the Behring Strait southward to the 51st parallel, and that this claim was protested against *in toto*, on the ground that the coast was almost entirely unoccupied, and that maritime jurisdiction, even where the coast was occupied, could not extend beyond 3 miles.

In the first Articles of the Conventions of 1824 and 1825 the claim to an extraordinary jurisdiction at sea was definitely abandoned, and the abandonment was a complete withdrawal of the claim made. It was principally against this very claim that the protests of Great Britain and the United States were directed, and its relinquishment was therefore, and purposely, placed at the head of each of the resulting Conventions.

Article I of the Convention between Russia and the United States is as follows:—

"It is agreed that in any part of the Great Ocean, commonly called the Pacific Ocean, or South Sea, the respective citizens or subjects of the High Contracting Powers shall be neither disturbed nor restrained, either in navigation or in fishing, or in the power of resorting to the coasts, upon points which may not already have been occupied, for the purpose of trading with the natives, saving always the restrictions and conditions determined by the following Articles."

Article I of the Convention between Great Britain and Russia is as follows:—

"It is agreed that the respective subjects of the High Contracting Parties shall not be troubled or molested in any part of the ocean, commonly called the Pacific Ocean, either in navigating the same, in fishing therein, or in landing at such parts of the coast as shall not have been already occupied, in order to trade with the natives, under the restrictions and conditions specified in the following Articles."

It has been contended, however, on the part of the United States, that the renunciation of claims contained in the Articles above quoted did not extend to what is now known as Behring Sea.

On this point Mr. Blaine, Secretary of State for the United States, writes:—

"The United States contends that the Behring Sea was not mentioned, or even referred to, in either Treaty, and was in no sense included in the phrase 'Pacific Ocean.' If Great Britain can maintain her position that the Behring Sea at the time of the Treaties with Russia of 1824 and 1825 was included in the Pacific Ocean, the Government of the United States has no well-grounded complaint against her."

In order to uphold the contention thus advanced by the United States, it is, however, further found necessary to maintain that the words "north-west coast" and "north-west coast of America," which frequently occur in the correspondence connected with those Conventions, refer only to a portion of the coast of the continent south of Behring Sea. This portion of the coast Mr. Blaine endeavours to define precisely in his letter, which has just been quoted, illustrating his meaning by maps, and seeking to restrict the application of the term to that part of the coast which runs southward continuously from the 60th parallel.

The meaning of the phrase "Pacific Ocean" and that of the term "north-west coast" are thus intimately associated in the contention of the United States, and it will be convenient to treat them together.

Meaning of the phrase "Pacific Ocean" and the term "North-west Coast" in the Treaties and Correspondence.

It will be found that such a construction of these phrases as Mr. Blaine has striven to place upon them cannot be reconciled with the correspondence.

In the first place, it has already been shown that Russia's object was not the acquisition of the control of the sea between Behring Strait and latitude 51°—this she distinctly denied—but the exclusion from her coasts in Asia and America, and on the islands, of the traders whose ventures threatened the success of the Russian-American Company.

No claim had been advanced by Russia which could possibly render a distinction between Behring Sea and the main Pacific of the slightest importance.

On the contrary, in the Ukase of 1799, Russia asserted jurisdiction over her subjects on all hunting grounds and establishments on the coast of America from the 55° north latitude to Behring Strait and thence southward to Japan,

---

Contention of the United States that Behring Sea was not included.

Mr. Blaine to Sir J. Pauncefote, Blue Book, "United States No. 1 (1891)." p. 37. See Appendix, vol. iii.

"North-west Coast."

Ibid., p. 38.

Meaning of "Pacific Ocean" and "North-west Coast" in the Treaties and correspondence.

M. de Poletica to Mr. Adams, February 28, 1822. See Appendix, vol. ii, Part II, No. 1.

and on the Aleutian, Kurile, and other Islands in all the "north-eastern" ocean.

In 1821, Russia was endeavouring to assert a title to the whole coast from Behring Strait to 51° north latitude on the American, and latitude 45° 50′ on the Asiatic coast.

Her claim to an extraordinary maritime jurisdiction over the non-territorial waters of the ocean was definitively abandoned at the outset of the negotiations, and the discussion was thenceforward confined to the protection of her rights within territorial limits.

Russia's object was the recognition and protection of the Russian Settlements in America. Accordingly, the Conventions provide against "illicit commerce," landing "at any place [from Behring Strait to the southernmost boundary] where there may be a Russian establishment without the permission of the Governor or Commandant," and against the formation of Establishments by either Power (in the respective Conventions) on territory claimed by, or conceded to, the other.

Usage of the terms in official correspondence.

See Appendix, vol. i, No. 1.

With the same object rules were made by Russia, headed "Rules established for the Limits of Navigation and Order of Communication along the coast of the Eastern Siberia, the *north-west-coast of America*, and the Aleutian, Kurile, and other Islands." This obviously included the American coast of Behring Sea in the term "north-west coast."

Ibid., vol. ii, Part I, No. 1.

Baron Nicolay, writing to Lord Londonderry, 31st October (12th November), 1821, says:—

" (Translation.)

"North-west Coast."

"The new Regulation does not forbid foreign vessels to navigate the seas which wash the Russian possessions on the *north-west coast of America* and the north-east coast of Asia.
    *   *   *

"On the other hand, in considering the Russian possessions which extend on the *north-west coast of America* from Behring Strait to 51° of north latitude, and also on the opposite coast of Asia and the adjacent islands, from the same Strait to 45°, &c.
    *   *   *

"Pacific Ocean."

"For, if it is demonstrated that the Imperial Government would, strictly speaking, have had the power to entirely close to foreigners that part of the *Pacific Ocean* on which our possessions in America and Asia border, there is all the more reason why the right, in virtue of which it has just adopted a measure much less generally restrictive, should not be called in question.
    *   *   *

"The officers commanding the Russian vessels of war,

which are to see to the maintenance of the above-mentioned arrangements in the *Pacific Ocean*, have been ordered to put them into force against those foreign vessels, &c."

In this note "north-west coast of America" is mentioned three times, and in each case the coast of Behring Sea is included in the term. "Pacific Ocean" appears twice, and in both instances includes the Behring Sea.

A map, published officially by Russian authorities, of which a copy is included among the documents annexed to this Case was forwarded from St. Petersburg by Sir Charles Bagot to Lord Londonderry, in a despatch dated the 17th November, 1821, in which it is thus described:— [For map, see Appendix, vol. iv, No 1. See Appendix, vol. ii, Part I, No. 4.]

"I have the honour to transmit to your Lordship, under a separate cover, an English translation of the Ukase, and I at the same time inclose a Map of the north-west coasts of America, and the Aleutian and Kurile Islands, which has been published in the Quartermaster-General's Department here, and upon which I have marked all the principal Russian Settlements.'

It will be seen on reference to this Map that the words "part of the north-west coast of America" include the whole coast line from a point north of Behring Straits down to latitude 54° north.

Again Lord Londonderry writes to Count Lieven:—

"The Undersigned has the honour hereby to acknowledge the note, addressed to him by Baron de Nicolay of the 12th November last, covering a copy of an Ukase issued by His Imperial Majesty the Emperor of All the Russias, and bearing date the 4th September, 1821, for various purposes, therein set forth, especially connected with the territorial rights of his Crown on the *north-western coast of America, bordering upon the Pacific*, and the commerce and navigation of His Imperial Majesty's subjects in the seas adjacent thereto." [Lord Londonderry to Count Lieven, January 18, 1822. See Appendix, vol. ii, Part I, No. 7.]

And Mr. S. Canning writing in February 1822 to Lord Londonderry from Washington, where he was then British Minister, observes:—

"I was informed this morning by Mr. Adams that the Russian Envoy has, within the last few days, communicated officially to the American Government an Ukase of the Emperor of Russia, which has lately appeared in the public prints, appropriating to the sovereignty and exclusive use of His Imperial Majesty the *north-west coast of America* down to the 51st parallel of latitude, together with a considerable portion of the opposite coasts of Asia, and the neighbouring seas to the extent of 100 Italian miles from any part of the coasts and intervening islands so appropriated. In apprizing me of this circumstance, Mr. Adams gave me to understand that it was not the intention of the American Cabinet to admit the claim thus [Mr. Stratford Canning to the Marquis of Londonderry, February 19, 1822. See Appendix, vol. ii, Part I, No. 9.]

"North-west Coast." notified on the part of Russia. His objection appears to lie more particularly against the exclusion of foreign vessels to so great a distance from the shore."

Again M. de Poletica, writing to Mr. Adams on the 28th February, 1822:—

See Appendix, vol. ii, Part II, No. 1.

"The first discoveries of the Russians on the north-west continent of America go back to the time of the Emperor Peter I. They belong to the attempt, made towards the end of the reign of this great Monarch, to find a passage from *the icy sea* into the *Pacific Ocean.*

* * * *

"When, in 1799, the Emperor Paul I granted to the present American Company its first Charter, he gave it the exclusive possession of the *north-west coast of America*, which belonged to Russia, from the 55th degree of north latitude to Behring Straits.

* * * *

"From this faithful exposition of known facts, it is easy, Sir, as appears to me, to draw the conclusion that the rights of Russia, to the extent of the *north-west coast*, specified in the Regulation of the Russian-American Company, rest, &c.

* * * *

"The Imperial Government, in assigning for limits to the *Russian possessions on the north-west coast of America, on the one side Behring Straits, and on the other the 51st degree* of north latitude, has, &c.

* * * *

"Pacific Ocean."

"I ought, in the last place, to request you to consider, Sir, that the *Russian possessions in the Pacific Ocean extend on the north-west coast of America from Behring Straits to the 51st degree of north latitude*, and on the opposite side of Asia and the islands adjacent from the same strait to the 45th degree."

Throughout this note the phrase "north-west coast" includes the coast of Behring Sea, and the last passage shows unmistakably that the Russians at that time regarded the Pacific Ocean as extending to Behring Strait.

The attention of the British Government was called to the Ukase by the Hudson's Bay Company in the following terms:—

"North-west Coast."

Hudson's Bay Company to the Marquis of Londonderry, March 27, 1822. See Appendix, vol. ii, Part I, No. 10.

"It has fallen under the observation of the Governor and Committee of the Hudson's Bay Company that the Russian Government have made a claim to the *north-west coast of America from Behring Straits* to the 51st degree of north latitude; and in an Imperial Ukase have prohibited foreign vessels from approaching the coast within 100 miles, under penalty of confiscation."

Mr. Adams to Mr. Rush, July 22, 1823. American State Papers, Foreign Relations, vol. v, p. 446. See Appendix, vol. ii, Part II, No. 4. See Appendix, vol. i, Nos. 3 and 4.

Mr. Adams, in 1823, dealt with the Russian claim as one of exclusive territorial right on the north-west coast of America, extending, as he said, from the "northern extremity of the continent." Articles in the "North American Review" (vol. xv, article 18), and "Quarterly Review" (1821-22, vol. xxvi, p. 344), published at the time of the controversy, and already referred to as mentioned with approbation by Mr. Adams, in 1824-25, use the words "north-west coast" with the same signification.

Mr. Adams, in his despatch of the 22nd July, 1823, to Mr. Middleton, referred to the Ukase of the Emperor Paul as purporting to grant to the American Company the "exclusive possession of the *north-west coast of America*, which belonged to Russia, from the 55th degree of *north latitude to Behring Strait*.

The fact that the whole, and not merely a particular portion, of the territorial and maritime claim advanced by the Ukase was in question, and was settled by the Treaties of 1824 and 1825 also appears from the Memorial laid by Mr. Middleton, on the part of the United States, before the Russian Government on the 17th December, 1823 :—

"North-west Coast."

American State Papers. Foreign Relations, vol. v, p. 436.
See Appendix, vol ii, Part II, No. 3.

"With all the respect which we owe to the declared intention and to the determination indicated by the Ukase, it is necessary to examine the two points of fact ; (1.) *If the country to the south and east of Behring Strait, as far as the 51st degree of north latitude, is found strictly unoccupied*. (2.) If there has been, latterly, a real occupation of this vast territory ? . . . . The conclusion which must necessarily result from these facts does not appear to establish that the territory in question had been legitimately incorporated with the Russian Empire.

"The extension of territorial rights to the distance of 100 miles from the coasts upon two opposite continents, and the prohibition of approaching to the same distance from these coasts, or from those of all the intervening islands, are innovations in the law of nations, and measures unexampled."

American State Papers, vol. v, p. 452.
See Appendix, vol. ii, Part II, No. 5.

In an earlier part of the same paper, Mr. Middleton observes :—

"The Ukase even goes to the *shutting up of a strait* which has never been till now shut up, and which is at present the principal object of discoveries, interesting and useful to the sciences.

"The very terms of the Ukase bear that this pretension has now been made for the first time."

The same appears from Mr. G. Canning's despatch to Sir C. Bagot of the 24th July, 1824 (which has been already quoted in another connection) :—

'Pacific Ocean.'

See Appendix, vol. ii, Part I, No. 44.

"Your Excellency will observe that there are but two points which have struck Count Lieven as susceptible of any question. The first, the assumption of the base of the mountains, instead of the summit as the line of boundary ; the second, the extension of the right *of navigation of the Pacific to the sea beyond Behring Straits.*

"Pacific Ocean."

See ante, p. 32.

"As o the second point, it is, perhaps, as Count Lieven remarks, new. But it is to be remarked, in return, that the circumstances under which this additional security is required will be new also.

"By the territorial demarcation agreed to in this 'Projet,' Russia will become possessed, in acknowledged sovereignty of both sides, of Behring Straits.

"The Power which could think of making the Pacific a *mare clausum* may not unnaturally be supposed capable of a disposition to apply the same character to a strait comprehended between two shores of which it becomes the undisputed owner; *but the shutting up of Behring Straits, or the power to shut them up hereafter, would be a thing not to be tolerated by England.*

"*Nor could we submit to be excluded, either positively or constructively, from a sea in which the skill and science of our seamen has been and is still employed in enterprises interesting not to this country alone, but to the whole civilized world.*

"The protection* given by the Convention to the American coasts of each Power may (if it is thought necessary) be extended in terms to the coasts of the Russian Asiatic territory; but in some way or other, if not in the form now prescribed, the free navigation of *Behring Straits, and of the seas beyond them,* must be secured to us."

It would have been of little advantage to secure the right to navigate through Behring Strait unless the right to navigate the sea leading to it was secured, which would not have been the case if the Ukase had remained in full force over Behring Sea.

The frequent references to Behring Strait and the seas beyond it show that there was no doubt in the minds of the British statesmen of that day that, in obtaining an acknowledgment of freedom of navigation and fishing throughout the Pacific, they had also secured this right as far as Behring Strait.

As corroborative proof of the usual practice of the British naval authorities, in the nomenclature of these waters, reference may be made to the instructions given in 1825 by the Lords Commissioners of the Admiralty, which will be found in the "Narrative of a Voyage to the Pacific and Behring Strait, &c.," under command of Captain F. W. Beechey, R.N., in the years 1825-26-27-28, published by authority in London, 1831.

These instructions from the Lords Commis-

---

* (*i.e.*) By the extension of territorial jurisdiction to two leagues, as originally proposed in the course of the negotiations between Great Britain and Russia.

sioners, which are full and detailed, make reference only to Behring Strait and the Pacific Ocean, and do not mention the Sea of Kamtchatka or Behring Sea.

Common meaning of "Pacific Ocean" and "North-West Coast."

The works of Mr. Robert Greenhow, Translator and Librarian to the United States' Department of State (well known in connection with the discussion of the "Oregon question"), afford a detailed and conclusive means of ascertaining the views officially held by the United States' Government on the meaning of *Pacific Ocean, Behring Sea, North-west coast,* and the extent to which the claims made by Russia in the Ukase of 1821 were abandoned by the Convention of 1824.

A "Memoir" was prepared by Mr. Greenhow, on the official request of Mr. L. F. Linn, Chairman of a Select Committee on the Territory of Oregon, by order of Mr. John Forsyth, Secretary of State. It includes a Map entitled "The North-west Coast of North America and adjacent Territories," which extends from below Acapulco in Mexico to above the mouth of the Kuskoquim in Behring Sea, and embraces also the greater part of the Aleutian chain.

Touching the signification of the terms *North-west coast* and *Pacific Ocean,* and the meaning attached to the relinquishment of Russian claims by the Convention of 1824, the first part of the "Memoir," under the heading "Geography of a Western Section of North America," contains the following passage:—

"The *north-west coast** is the expression usually employed in the United States at the present time to distinguish the vast portion of the American continent which extends north of the 40th parallel of latitude from the Pacific to the great dividing ridge of the *Rocky Mountains,* together with the contiguous islands in that ocean. The southern part of this territory, which is drained almost entirely by the River Columbia, is commonly called *Oregon,* from the supposition (no doubt erroneous) that such was the name applied to its principal stream by the aborigines. To the more northern parts of the continent many appellations, which will hereafter be mentioned, have been assigned by navigators and fur traders of various nations. The territory bordering upon the Pacific southward, from the 40th parallel to the

* N.B.—The *italics* in this and subsequent quotations are those employed by Greenhow himself.

Common meaning of "Pacific Ocean" and "North-west Coast."

Greenhow's works.

"Memoir Historical and Political of the north-west coast of North America and the adjacent territories, illustrated by a Map and a geographical view of these countries, by Robert Greenhow, Translator and Librarian to the Department of State." Senate, 26th Cong., 1st Session (174), 1840. The same Memoir, separately printed apparently in identical form, and with the same Map and pagination Wiley & Putnam, New York, 1840.

"North-west Coast."

extremity of the peninsula which stretches in that direction as far as the Tropic of Cancer, is called *California*, a name of uncertain derivation, formerly applied by the Spaniards to the whole western section of North America, as that of *Florida* was employed by them to designate the regions bordering upon the Atlantic. The north-west coast and the west coast of California together form the *west coast of North America;* as it has been found impossible to separate the history of these two portions, so it will be necessary to include them both in this geographical view." (p. 1).

Mr. Greenhow here gives the following note:—

"In the following pages the term *coast* will be used, sometimes as signifying only the sea-shore, and sometimes as embracing the whole territory, extending therefrom to the sources of the river; care has been, however, taken to prevent misapprehension, where the context does not sufficiently indicate the true sense. In order to avoid repetitions, the *north-west coast* will be understood to be the north-west coast *of North America;* all *latitudes* will be taken as *north latitudes,* and all *longitudes* as *west from Greenwich,* unless otherwise expressed."

The "Memoir" continues as follows:—

"Pacific Ocean."

"The northern extremity of the west coast of America is *Cape Prince of Wales,* in latitude of 65° 52′, which is also the westernmost spot in the whole continent; it is situated on the eastern side of *Beering's Strait,* a channel 51 miles in width, connecting the Pacific with the *Arctic* [or *Icy* or *North Frozen*] *Ocean,* on the western side of which strait, opposite Cape Prince of Wales, is *East Cape,* the eastern extremity of Asia. Beyond Beering Strait the shores of the two continents recede from each other. The *north coast of America* has been traced from Cape Prince of Wales north-eastward to *Cape Barrow,*" &c. (pp. 3-4).

The relations of Behring Sea to the Pacific Ocean are defined as follows in the "Memoir":—

"The part of the Pacific north of the Aleutian Islands which bathes those shores is commonly distinguished as the *Sea of Kamtchatka,* and sometimes as *Behring Sea,* in honour of the Russian navigator of that name who first explored it " (pp. 4-5).

(Geography of Oregon and California and the other parts on the north-west coast of North America." York, 1845.

Again, in the "Geography of Oregon and California," Mr. Greenhow writes:—

"Cape Prince of Wales, the westernmost point of America, is the eastern pillar of Behring Strait, a passage only 50 miles in width, separating that continent from Asia, and forming the only direct communication between the Pacific and Arctic Oceans.

* * * *

"The part of the Pacific called the *Sea of Kamtchatka*, or Behring Sea, north of the Aleutian chain, likewise contains several islands," &c. (p. 4).

Greenhow's "History" was officially presented to the Government of Great Britain by the Government of the United States in July 1845, in connection with the Oregon discussion and in pursuance of an Act of Congress.*

In this History the Sea of Kamtchatka, or Behring's Sea, is again referred to as a part of the Pacific Ocean.

In respect of the understanding by the United States that the claims advanced by the Ukase of 1821 had been entirely relinquished by the Russian and United States' Convention of 1824,

"Pacific Ocean."

"The History of Oregon and California and the other territories on the north-west coast of North America, by Robert Greenhow, Translator and Librarian to the Department of State of the United States; author of a Memoir, Historical and Political on the north-west coast of North America, published in 1840 by direction of the Senate of the United States." New York, 1845.
This is a second edition, and in the preface it is explained that its issue was rendered necessary to supply 1,500 copies of the work which had been ordered for the General Government.
The same work. First edition, London, 1844.
Both editions contain Maps, which appear to be identical, but different from the Maps accompanying the Memoir, though including nearly the same limits with them.

---

* The following is the correspondence accompanying the presentation by the Government of the United States:—

"*Mr. Buchanan to Mr. Pakenham.*

"*Department of State, Washington,*
"Sir, "*July* 12, 1845.

"In pursuance of an Act of Congress approved on the 20th February, 1845, I have the honour to transmit to you herewith, for presentation to the Government of Great Britain, one copy of the 'History of Oregon, California, and the other territories on the North-west Coast of America,' by Robert Greenhow, Esq., Translator and Librarian of the Department of State.
"I avail, &c.
(Signed) "JAMES BUCHANAN."

"*Mr. Pakenham to the Earl of Aberdeen.*—(*Received August* 16.)

"My Lord, "*Washington, July* 29, 1845.
"I have the honour herewith to transmit a copy of a note which I have received from the Secretary of State of the United States, accompanied by a copy of Mr. Greenhow's work on Oregon and California, which, in pursuance of an Act of Congress, is presented to Her Majesty's Government.

"Although Mr. Greenhow's book is already in your Lordship's possession, I think it right, in consequence of the official character with which it is presented, to forward to your Lordship the inclosed volume, being the identical one which has been sent to me by Mr. Buchanan.

"I have not failed to acknowledge the receipt of Mr. Buchanan's note in suitable terms.
"I have, &c.
(Signed) "R. PAKENHAM."

the following is found on a later page of the volume last referred to:—

"This Convention does not appear to offer any grounds for dispute as to the construction of its stipulations, but is, on the contrary, clear, and equally favourable to both nations. The rights of both parties to navigate every part of the Pacific, and to trade with the natives of any places on the coasts of that sea, not already occupied, are first distinctly acknowledged, &c." (p. 342).

It is thus clear, as the result of the investigations undertaken by Greenhow on behalf of the United States' Government—

That Behring Sea was a part of the Pacific.

That the north-west coast was understood to extend to Behring Strait.

That Russia relinquished her asserted claims over "every part of the Pacific."

Russian interpretation of "Pacific Ocean."

That the phrase "Pacific Ocean" in the Treaty included Behring Sea is still further shown by the reply of the Russian Government to Governor Etholin in 1842, when he wished to keep American whalers out of Behring Sea:—

Tikhmenieff. See Appendix, vol i, No. 5.

"The claim to a *mare clausum*, if we wished to advance such a claim in respect to the *northern part of the Pacific Ocean*, could not be theoretically justified. *Under Article I of the Convention of 1824 between Russia and the United States, which is still in force, American citizens have a right to fish in all parts of the Pacific Ocean.* But under Article IV of the same Convention, the ten years' period mentioned in that Article having expired, we have power to forbid American vessels to visit inland seas, gulfs, harbours, and bays for the purposes of fishing and trading with the natives. That is the limit of our rights, and we have no power to prevent American ships from taking whales in the open sea."

1846. *Ibid*

Again, in the reply of the Russian Government to representations of the Governor-General of Eastern Siberia in 1846, the following words occur:—

"We have no right to exclude foreign ships from *that part of the great ocean* which separates the eastern shore of Siberia from the north-western shore of America," &c.

The instructions which were finally issued to the Russian cruizers on the 9th December, 1853, are to the same effect.

Interpretation in the United States.

See post, p. 99.

The Legislature of the Territory of Washington, in 1866, referred to "fishing banks known to navigators to exist along the Pacific coast from the Cortes bank to Behring Strait."

It is clear that the Honourable Charles Sumner, when proposing to the Senate, in the year 1867, the adoption of the Treaty of Cession of Alaska, understood the words "North Pacific" in the sense in which these words are defined by the authorities just cited. In his speech on that occasion, Mr. Sumner thus referred to the waters in question:—

"Sea-otter seems to belong exclusively to the North Pacific. . . . . . Its present zone is between the parallels of 60° and 65° north latitude on the American and Asiatic coasts, so that its range is very limited." See Appendix, vol. I, No. 6.

Mr. H. W. Elliott, who was engaged in the study of the seal islands of Alaska for the United States' Government as late as the year 1881, in his official Report on the seal islands of Alaska remarks, concerning the seals:— Report on the Seal Islands of Alaska, Washington, 1881, pp. 6, 7.

"Their range *in the North Pacific* is virtually confined to four islands in Bering Sea, namely, St. Paul and St. George, of the tiny Pribyloff group, and Bering and Copper of the Commander Islands."

Again, he says:—

"In the North Atlantic no suitable territory for their reception exists, or ever did exist; and really nothing *in the North Pacific* beyond what we have designated in Bering Sea."

He also describes the rookeries in Behring Sea as "North Pacific rookeries."

And writes further:—

"Geographically, as well as in regard to natural history, Bering Island is one of the most curious islands in the *northern part of the Pacific Ocean.*" Ibid, p. 110.

The above are, however, only a few from among very many similar instances which might be quoted of the continued usage of the name "Pacific Ocean" as including Behring Sea.

In 1882, a Notice which affected part of Okhotsk and Behring Seas was published by A. K. Pelikan, His Royal and Imperial Majesty's Consul, Yokohama, on the 15th November, 1881, from which the following is an extract:—

"At the request of the local authorities of Behring and other islands, the Undersigned hereby notifies that the Russian Imperial Government publishes for general knowledge the following:— 50th Cong., 2nd Sess., Sen. Ex. Doc. No. 106, p 259.

Pacific.

"'1. Without a special permit or licence from the Governor-General of Eastern Siberia, foreign vessels are not allowed to carry on trading, hunting, fishing, &c., on the Russian coast or islands in the Okhotsk and Behring Seas, or on the north-eastern coast of Asia, or within their sea boundary-line.'"

In the correspondence between the United States and Russia, touching the meaning of this Regulation, the Notice is alluded to by M. de Giers as "relative to fishing, hunting, and to trade in the Russian waters of the Pacific," and as relative to fishing and hunting in "our Pacific waters."

In the same correspondence the Secretary of State of the United States and the United States' Minister at St. Petersburg similarly speak of "Pacific Coast fisheries" and "our Pacific Ocean fisheries."

Writing on the 8th (20th) May, 1882, to Mr. Hoffman, the American Minister at St. Petersburg, M. de Giers said:—

50th Cong., 2nd Sess., Senate Ex. Doc. No. 106, p. 282.
See Appendix, vol. ii, Part II, No. 16.

"Referring to the exchange of communications which has taken place between us on the subject of a Notice published by our Consul at Yokohama relative to fishing, hunting, and to trade *in the Russian waters of the Pacific*, and in reply to the note which you addressed to me, dated the 15th (27th) March, I am now in a position to give you the following information:—

"A Notice of the tenour of that annexed to your note of the 15th March was, in fact, published by our Consul at Yokohama, and our Consul-General at San Francisco is also authorized to publish it.

"This measure refers only to prohibited industries and to the trade in contraband; the restrictions which it establishes extend strictly to the territorial waters of Russia only. It was required by the numerous abuses proved in late years, and which fell with all their weight on the population of our sea-shore and of our islands, whose only means of support is by fishing and hunting. These abuses inflicted also a marked injury on the interests of the Company to which the Imperial Government had conceded the monopoly of fishing and hunting ('exportation'), in islands called the 'Commodore' and the 'Seals.'

"Beyond this new Regulation, of which the essential point is the obligation imposed upon captains of vessels who desire to fish and to hunt in the *Russian waters of the Pacific* to provide themselves at Vladivostock with the permission or licence of the Governor-General of Oriental Siberia, the right of fishing, hunting, and of trade by foreigners in our territorial waters is regulated by Article 560, and those following, of vol. xii, Part II, of the Code of Laws.

"Informing you of the preceding, I have, &c."

[248] L

Bancroft writes, in his "History of Alaska" (pp. 19, 20): "The Anadir, which empties into the Pacific." Again: "Thus the Pacific Ocean was first reached by the Russians on the shore of the Okhotsk Sea." And yet again: "The ascent of the Lena brought the Russians to Lake Baikal, and showed them another route to the Pacific, through China by way of the Amoor."

So, in 1887, it is found that the American Representative at St. Petersburg informed Mr. Bayard (17th February, 1887) that the Notice already quoted prohibits fishing, &c., on "the Russian Pacific coasts." This correspondence related to a seizure which had been made in Behring Straits.

"Pacific."

50th Cong., 2nd Sess., Senate Ex. Doc. No. 106, p. 268. See Appendix, vol. ii, Part II, No. 18.

Geographical use of "Pacific Ocean" and "North-West Coast."

In the discussion of the question of jurisdiction between the United States and Great Britain special reference has been made by the United States to the marking of Maps, from which it has been insisted that the waters of Behring Sea had been given a name distinct from that of the Pacific Ocean.

From this it was urged that the words "Pacific Ocean" in the Conventions were used with great care, so as to reserve under the exclusive jurisdiction of Russia the waters of Behring Sea.

It is, however, to be noted in studying any series of Maps chronologically arranged, particularly those published before the middle of the present century, that Behring Sea is frequently without any special name, though the adjoining Sea of Okhotsk is in almost every instance clearly designated.

On various Charts issued by the United States' Hydrographic Office, including the latest and most perfect editions now in actual use, the expression "Pacific" or "North Pacific Ocean" is used as including Behring Sea. This appears from the titles of such Charts, of which the following may be referred to:—

No. 909. Published March 1883 at the Hydrographic Office, Washington, D.C.:—

"Pacific Ocean. Behring Sea, Plover Bay, from a survey by Lieutenant Maximov, Imperial Russian Navy, 1876."

(Plover Bay is situated on the Asiatic coast, near the entrance to Behring Strait.)

Geographical use of "Pacific Ocean" and "North-west Coast."

"Pacific" and "North-west Coast" in geographical works.

No. 010. Published October 1882 at the Hydrographic Office, Washington, D.C.:—
"North Pacific Ocean. Anadir Bay, Behring Sea. From a Chart by Engineer Bulkley, of New York, in 1865," &c.
(Anadir Bay is situated between latitudes 64° and 65° on the Asiatic side of Behring Sea.)

Similar evidence is afforded by the title-page of the work issued by the same Hydrographic Office in 1869, as follows:—
"Directory of Behring Sea and the coast of Alaska. . . . . Arranged from the Directory of the Pacific Ocean."

The British Admiralty Chart of Behring Sea, corrected up to November 1889, but originally compiled in 1884 (No. 2400), is likewise entitled as follows:—
"North-west Pacific. Kamchatka to Kadiak Island, including Behring Sea and Strait."

The definitions touching the Pacific Ocean, Behring Sea, &c., to be found in gazetteers, dictionaries, and geographical works, both of the present and past dates, moreover, show conclusively that Behring Sea was, at the time of the Conventions, and is now, understood to form an integral part of the Pacific Ocean.

Such formal definitions are naturally more trustworthy than inferences drawn from the construction of Maps.

A few of these will suffice, though many more might be quoted :—

Shaw, John, "Naval Gazetteer," London, 1795.

"Beering's Straits, which is the passage from the North Pacific Ocean to the Arctic Sea."

Brookes, R., "General Gazetteer," 12th ed., London, 1802.

"Beering's Island. An island in the Pacific Ocean."
"Kamschatka. Bounded east and south by Pacific."

Bölti, J. G. A., "Allgemeines Geographisches Wörterbuch," Pesth, 1822.

"Stilles Meer. Vom 5 nordl. Br. an bis zur Beringsstrasse aufwarts stets heftige Sturme."

Dictionnaire Géographique Universel," Tom. iv, Paris, 33-39.

"Mer Pacifique. Il s'étend du nord au sud depuis le Cercle Polaire Arctique, c'est-à-dire, depuis le Détroit de Behring, qui le fait communiquer à l'Océan Glacial Austral."

Dr. J. C., "Geographisches Statistisches Handwörterbuch," Bd. iii, Pesth, 1822, Halberstadt, 1829.

"Stilles Meer. Vom 30 südlicher Breite bis zum 5 nördlicher Breite verdient es durch seine Heiterkeit und Stille den namen des Stillen Meers; von da an bis zur Beringsstrasse ist es heftigen Stürmen unterworfen."

Smith, "Grammar of Modern Geography," London,

"Bhering's Strait connects the Frozen Ocean with the Pacific.
"The Anadir flows into the Pacific Ocean.
"The principal gulfs of Asiatic Russia are: the Gulf of Anadir, near Bhering's Strait; the Sea of Penjina, and the Gulf of Okhotsk, between Kamtchatka and the mainland of Russia—all three in the Pacific Ocean."

"L'Océan Pacifique Boréal s'étend depuis le Détroit de Behring jusqu'au Tropique de Cancer." — "Précis de la Géographie Universelle," par Mal e-Brun, Tom. II, p. 181, Paris, 1831-37.

"Le Détroit de Behring. A commencer par ce détroit le Grand Océan (ou Océan Pacifique) forme la limite orientale de l'Asie." — Ibid., Tom. viii, p. 4.

"Behring (détroit célèbre). Il joint Océan Glacial Arctique au Grand Océan." — Langlois, "Dictionnaire de Géographie," T. m. I, Paris, 1838.

"The Pacific Ocean. Its boundary-line is pretty well determined by the adjacent continents, which approach one another towards the north, and at Behring's Strait which separates them, are only about 36 miles apart. This strait may be considered as closing the Pacific on the north." — "Penny Cyclopædia," vol xvii, London, 1910.

"Behring (Détroit de) à l'extrémité nord-est de l'Asie, sépare ce continent de l'Amérique et l'Océan Glacial Arctique de l'Océan Pacifique." — "Dictionnaire Universel d'Histoire et de Géographie," par M. N. Bouillet, Paris, 1842.

"Behring (Mer de), partie de l'Océan Pacifique."

"Behring (Détroit de). Canal de l'Océan .... unissant les eaux de l'Océan Pacifique à celles de l'Océan Arctique." — "Dictionnaire Géographique et Statistique," par Adr. Golbert. Tom. I, Paris, 1850.

"Pacific Ocean. Between longitude 70° west and 110° east, that is, for a space of over 180°, it covers the greater part of the earth's surface, from Behring's Straits to the Polar Circle, that separates it from the Antarctic Ocean." — "The New American Cyclopædia," edited by Geo. Ripley and Charles A. Dana, New York, 1861.

"Behring Sea is that part of the North Pacific Ocean between the Aleutian Islands in latitude 55° north and Behring Strait in latitude 66° north, by which latter it communicates with the Arctic Ocean." — "Harper's Statistical Gazetteer of the World," vol. i, J. Collins Smith, New York, 1855.

"Behring Sea, sometimes called the Sea of Kamtchatka, is that portion of the North Pacific Ocean lying between the Aleutian Islands and Behring's Strait." — "Imperial Gazetteer," vol. I, Glasgow, 1856.

"Behring (Détroit de). Canal du Grand Océan unissant les eaux de l'Océan Pacifique à celles de l'Océan Glacial Arctique." — "Grand Dictionnaire de Géographie Universelle," S. N. Deseberelle, Tom. I, Paris, 1856-57.

"Pacific Ocean. Its extreme southern limit is the Antarctic Circle, from which it stretches northward through 132° of latitude to Behring's Strait, which separates it from the Arctic Ocean." — McCulloch's "Geographical Dictionary," edited by Martin, vol. iii, London, 1866.

"Behring (Détroit de). Canal ou bras de mer unissant les eaux de l'Océan Glacial Arctique à celles de l'Océan Pacifique." — "Grand Dictionnaire Universel," par P. La R., Tom. II, Paris, 1866-76.

"Behring (Détroit de). Passage qui unit l'Océan Glacial Arctique au Grand Océan." — St. Martin, "Nouveau Dictionnaire de Géographie Universelle," Tom. I, Paris, 1879.

"Behring Sea, or Sea of Kamchatka, is that part of the North Pacific Ocean between the Aleutian Islands in latitude 55° north and Behring Strait in latitude 66° north, by which latter it communicates with the Arctic Ocean." — Lippincott's "Gazetteer of the World," Philadelphia.

"Beringsstrasse. Meerenge das nordöstlichste Eismeer mit dem Stillen Ocean verbindend." — Ritter's "Geographisch Statistisch Lexicon," Ed. i, 1883.

"Behring's Strait, connecting the North Pacific with the Arctic Ocean." — Blackie's "Modern Cyclopædia," vol. I, London, edition.

"Behring's Sea, sometimes called the Sea of Kamchatka, is that portion of the North Pacific Ocean lying between the Aleutian Islands and Behring's Strait."

Views of English and American Jurists.

Finally, a few passages may be quoted from English and American publicists of acknowledged eminence, to show the manner in which the general question has been viewed by them.

Woolsey, "Introduction to International Law," 3rd edit'on, New York, 1872, p. 63.

Dr. T. D. Woolsey, President of Yale College, "Introduction to the Study of International Law," 3rd edition, New York, 1872, p. 63 :—

"Russia, finally, at a more recent date, based an exclusive claim to the Pacific, north of the 51st degree, upon the ground that this part of the ocean was a passage to shores lying exclusively within her jurisdiction. But this claim was resisted by our government, and withdrawn in the temporary convention of 1824. A treaty of the same empire with Great Britain in 1825 contains similar concessions."

Wharton, "Digest of International Law," Washington, 1886, vol. i, section 32, p 3.

In referring to the Russian Ukase of 1821, Wharton, "Digest of International Law of the United States," Washington, 1886, vol. i, section 32, p. 3, speaks of Russia—

"Having asserted in 1822 to 1824 an exclusive jurisdiction over the *north-west coast and waters of America from Behring Strait to the fifty-first degree of north latitude.*"

Davis, "Outlines of International Law," New York, 1887, p. 44.

Mr. Davis, Assistant Professor of Law at the United States' Military Academy, "Outlines of International Law," New York, 1887, p. 44 :—

"Russia, in 1822, laid claim to exclusive jurisdiction over that part of the Pacific Ocean lying north of the 51st degree of north latitude, on the ground that it possessed the shores of that sea on both continents beyond that limit, and so had the right to restrict commerce to the coast inhabitants."

A recent United States' writer, Professor J. B. Angell, discussing this subject, says :—

Jas. B. Angell, in the 'Forum,' November 1889; "American Rights in Behring Sea."

See Appendix, vol. i, No. 8.

"The Treaty of 1824 secured to us the right of navigation and fishing 'in any part of the great ocean, commonly called the Pacific Ocean, or South Sea, and (in Article IV) for ten years that of frequenting the interior seas, gulfs, harbours, and creeks upon the coast for the purpose of fishing and trading. At the expiration of ten years Russia refused to renew this last provision, and it never was formally renewed. But, for nearly fifty years at least, American vessels have been engaged in taking whales in Behring Sea without being disturbed by the Russian Government. Long before the cession of Alaska to us, hundreds of our whaling vessels annually visited the Arctic Ocean and Behring Sea, and brought home rich cargoes. It would seem, therefore, that Russia regarded Behring Sea as a part of the Pacific Ocean, and not as one of the 'interior seas,' access to which was forbidden by the termination of the IVth Article of the Treaty."

Sir R. Phillimore, in the 2nd edition of "Commentaries upon International Law," vol. i, p. 241, remarks :— *Phillimore, "International Law," 2nd edition, vol. i, p. 241 [3rd edition, p. 290].*

"In 1822 Russia laid claim to a sovereignty over the Pacific Ocean north of the 51st degree of latitude ; but the Government of the United States of America resisted this claim as contrary to the principles of international law."

Mr. W. E. Hall, "Principles of International Law," Clarendon Press, Oxford, 3rd edition, 1890, p. 147 :— *Hall, "International Law," 3rd edition, p. 147.*

"*Note.*—A new claim subsequently sprung up in the Pacific, but it was abandoned in a very short time. The Russian Government pretended to be Sovereign over the Pacific north of the 51st degree of latitude, and published an Ukase in 1821 prohibiting foreign vessels from approaching within 100 Italian miles of the coasts and islands bordering upon or included in that portion of the ocean. This pretension was resisted by the United States and Great Britain, and was wholly given up by Conventions between the former Powers and Russia in 1824 and 1825."

The arguments contained in the foregoing chapter establish :—

That the Treaty of 1825 between Great Britain and Russia applied, and was intended to apply, to all the non-territorial waters of the North Pacific, extending from Behring Strait upon the north to latitude 54° upon the coast of America, and to latitude 45° 50' upon the coast of Asia (being the whole extent of sea covered by the Ukase).

That at no stage of the controversy was any distinction drawn, or intended to be drawn, between the seas to the north and the seas to the south of the Aleutian Islands.

That Behring Sea was included in the phrase "Pacific Ocean" as used in the Treaty of 1825.

That the expression "north-west coast of America," or, in its abbreviated form, "north-west coast," included the coast up to Behring Strait.

CHAPTER IV.

HEAD (D).—*The User of the Waters in question from 1821 to 1867.*

User of Waters from 1821 to 1867.

As regards the user of the waters in question, it has been shown that down to the year 1821 Russia made no attempt in practice to assert or exercise jurisdiction over foreign vessels when beyond the ordinary territorial jurisdiction. With the exception of the incidents connected with the Ukase of 1821, already referred to in Chapter II, the same is true of the period between 1821 and 1867.

Historical Outline.

To resume the historical statement in chronological order:—

1821. Alaska, pp. 534, 535.

In the year 1821 Mouravief was sent out to take control at Sitka under the new Charter. He assumed the name of "Governor" in place of that of "Chief Manager," which had previously been employed.

North-west Coast, vol. i, pp. 340, 341.

The names of seven trading-vessels on the north-west coast are known for this year.*

1822. Alaska, pp. 537–539.

In 1822, the Russian vessel "Rurik" arrived at Sitka from Kronstadt with supplies. About the close of the year the Russian sloop-of-war "Apollon" also arrived, with instructions that all trade with foreigners should cease. This interdict remained in force for two years, and seriously interfered with the profits of the Company.

Ibid., p. 540.

In this year also the Russian sloops-of-war "Kreisser" and "Ladoga" arrived to enforce the provisions of the Ukase, and remained for two years.

Ibid., p. 540.

An exploratory expedition, which remained absent two years, was dispatched from Sitka to the eastern shore of Behring Sea.

1823. Ibid., pp. 536–539.

In 1823, a famine was feared at Sitka and on the coast, and the "Rurik" and an American vessel which had been purchased, were sent to California and the Sandwich Islands for supplies.

Referring to this incident, Bancroft writes:—

Ibid., p. 538.

"As in this instance, the Colonies had frequently been relieved from want by trade with foreigners; and, indeed,

* See note on p. 19 referring to trading-vessels on the north-west coast. None of these trading-vessels were Russian.

this was too often the only means of averting starvation. Even between 1818 and 1822, when supplies were comparatively abundant, goods, consisting mainly of provisions, were obtained by traffic with American and English coasters to the value of more than 300,000 roubles in scrip."

In the same year, the "Rob Roy," from Boston, is known to have been on the north-west coast. North-west Coast, vol i, p. 341.

In 1824, Kotzebue, in the "Predpriatie," called at Sitka. About this time the shareholders of the Russian Company protested against the interdict of foreign trade, and Sitka was, in consequence, again opened to such trade. Alaska, p. 540. Ibid., p. 541.

1824.

Acting under the authority of the Ukase of 1821, the United States' brig "Pearl," when on a voyage from Boston to Sitka, had been in the year 1822 seized by the Russian sloop "Apollon." Count Nesselrode, in his despatch to Count Lieven (26th June, 1823), when communicating the suspension of the Ukase of 1821, says the advices to this effect were sent from St. Petersburg in August of 1823, and that the officer of the "Apollon" could not receive them before September 1824, and that, therefore, he could not have known of them at the "time of the occurrence of the incident reported by the American press." Dall's Alaska, pp. 233, 234.
See Appendix, vol. ii, Part I, No. 20.

In 1824, the "Pearl" was released, and compensation was paid for her arrest and detention. As to the "Pearl," see S. Canning to G. Canning, April 23, 1823. Appendix, vol. ii, Part I, No. 24.

In the same year four vessels are recorded as having visited the north-west coast, and some of them are known to have repeated their visits in later years. North-west Coast, vol. i, p. 341.

In 1825, the "Elena" arrived at Sitka with supplies. Kotzebue also again called at Sitka. Alaska, p. 539.

1825

Remonstrances were addressed by the Russian-American Company to the Russian Government as to the effect of the Conventions of 1824 and 1825. The name of but one vessel trading on the north-west coast has been preserved in this year. Ibid., p. 544.
North-west Coast, vol. i, p. 341.

In 1826, Chistiakof wrote to the Directors of the Company, asking that an experienced whaling master should be sent out. In July of this year Her Majesty's ship "Blossom," under Captain Beechey, sailed through Behring Sea into the Arctic Ocean. Alaska, p. 562.
Beechey's Voyage to the Pacific and Behring Strait, London, 1831, vol. ii, p. 335.

1826.

1827.	Alaska, p. 546.	In 1827, Lütke, sent by the Russian Government, arrived at Sitka, and thereafter made explorations in the Aleutian Islands and in Behring Sea.
	North-west Coast, vol. i, p. 341.	Two vessels only of the trading fleet on the north-west coast are in this year known by name.
1828.	Alaska, p. 546.'	In 1828, two vessels belonging to Lütke's expedition carried on surveys in Behring Sea. The trading-vessel "Eliza" was at Sitka in this year.
	Letter of Brewer to Amory, H.R., Ex. Doc., 40th Cong, 2nd Sess., No. 177, p. 85.	In the years 1826, 1827, and 1828 the "Chinchella," a United States' brig, Thomas Meek, master, was trading between Sitka and China.
1829.	Alaska, p. 565.	In 1829, a Russian vessel was sent from Sitka to Chile to trade. Some explorations were also made by the Russians in the inland country.
1830.	Ibid., p. 547.	In 1830, explorations were made in Behring Sea by Etholen. Wrangell relieved Chistiakof in command. The names of four or five foreign vessels trading on the north-west coast in this and the following year are recorded.
	North-west Coast, vol. i, p 341.	
1832 or 1833.	Alaska, pp. 548-552.	In 1832 or 1833, Tebenkof established a post near the mouth of the Yukon, and explorations were conducted inland.
1833.	Ibid., p. 555.	In 1833, the Hudson's Bay Company sent the British vessel "Dryad" to form an Establishment at the mouth of the Stikine, but Wrangell, having heard of the enterprise, occupied the place in advance, and turned the vessel back. Damages to the amount of 20,000l. were claimed through the British Government from Russia. This will be referred to later.
	See post, p. 83.	
	Ibid., p. 583.	A United States' whaling master, under a five-years' Contract with the Russian Company, arrived at Sitka, but achieved little.
1834.	North-west Coast, vol. i, p. 341.	In 1834, the name of but one of the foreign vessels trading on the north-west coast is recorded.
1836.	Ibid., pp. 341, 342.	In 1836, the "Eliza" was again at Sitka, and three foreign trading-vessels are recorded to have visited the Alaskan coast.

The case of the "Loriot."

Case of the "Loriot."

In the same year the United States' brig "Loriot" sailed from the Sandwich Islands for the north-west coast of America for the purpose of procuring provisions, and also Indians to hunt for sea-otters on the coast. When in the Harbour of Tuckessan, latitude 54° 55' north, and longitude 132° 30' west, a Russian armed brig ordered the "Loriot" to leave. This action was based on the expiration of the period named in the IVth Article of the Treaty, whereby, for ten years only, liberty to touch and trade at Russian Establishments on the coast was granted.

The United States protested against the interference with the "Loriot," characterizing it as an "outrage," and the following is an extract from instructions which were sent by the United States' Secretary of State to Mr. Dallas, the Minister at St. Petersburg, under date 4th May, 1837:—

Case of the "Loriot."

40th Cong., 2nd Sess., Senate, Ex. Doc. No. 106, p. 233.
See Appendix, vol. ii, Part II, No. 6.

"On the other hand, should there prove to be no Russian Establishments at the places mentioned, this outrage on the 'Loriot' assumes a still graver aspect. It is a violation of the right of the citizens of the United States, immemorially exercised, and secured to them as well by the law of nations as by the stipulations of the 1st Article of the Convention of 1824, to fish in those seas, and to resort to the coast, for the prosecution of their lawful commerce upon points not already occupied. As such it is the President's wish that you should remonstrate, in an earnest but respectful tone, against this groundless assumption of the Russian Fur Company, and claim from His Imperial Majesty's Government for the owners of the brig 'Loriot,' for their losses and for the damages they have sustained, such indemnification as may, on an investigation of the case, be found to be justly due to them."

Mr. Dallas subsequently wrote that he was led to believe that Russian Establishments had been made at the places mentioned. Nevertheless, the United States contended that at the expiration of the IVth Article, the law of nations practically gave United States' ships the privileges therein mentioned.

50th Cong., 2nd Sess., Senate Ex. Doc. No. 106, p. 234.
See Appendix, vol. ii, Part II, No. 7.
Ibid., p. 226.
See Appendix, vol. ii, Part II, No 8.

Mr. Dallas (16th August, 1837) wrote to the Secretary of State:—

"The 1st Article asserts for both countries general and permanent rights of navigation, fishing, and trading with the natives, upon points not occupied by either, north or south of the agreed parallel of latitude."

Ibid., p. 234.
See Appendix, vol. ii, Part II, No. 7.

Mr. Forsyth, Secretary of State for the United States, writing to Mr. Dallas on the 3rd November, 1837, and referring to the 1st Article of the

Ibid., p. 236.
See Appendix, vol. ii, Part II, No. 9

Case of the "Loriot."

Convention of April 1824 between the United States and Russia, said:—

"The 1st Article of that instrument is only declaratory of a right which the parties to it possessed under the law of nations without conventional stipulations, to wit, to navigate and fish in the ocean upon an unoccupied coast, and to resort to such coast for the purpose of trading with the natives.

* * * *

"The United States, in agreeing not to form new establishments to the north of latitude of 54° 40′ N., made no acknowledgment of the right of Russia to the territory above that line."

And, again:—

"It cannot follow that the United States ever intended to abandon the just right acknowledged by the 1st Article to belong to them under the law of nations—to frequent any part of the unoccupied coast of North America for the purpose of fishing or trading with the natives. All that the Convention admits is an inference of the right of Russia to acquire possession by settlement north of 54° 40′ N. Until that actual possession is taken, the 1st Article of the Convention acknowledges the right of the United States to fish and trade as prior to its negotiations."

50th Cong., 2nd Sess., Senate Ex. Doc. No. 106, p. 238.
See Appendix, vol. ii, Part II, No. 10.

In his despatch of the 23rd February, 1838, Count Nesselrode, the Russian Foreign Minister, wrote to Mr. Dallas:—

"It is true, indeed, the 1st Article of the Convention of 1824, to which the proprietors of the 'Loriot' appeal, secures to the citizens of the United States entire liberty of navigation in the Pacific Ocean, as well as the right of landing without disturbance upon all points on the north-west coast of America, not already occupied, and to trade with the natives."

Again, Mr. Dallas, in a despatch to Count Nesselrode, dated the 5th (17th) March, 1838, interpreted Article 1 of the Convention as being applicable to *any part of the Pacific Ocean*. He wrote:—

Ibid., p. 241.
See Appendix, vol. ii, Part II, No. 11.

". . . . The right of the citizens of the United States to navigate the Pacific Ocean, and their right to trade with the aboriginal natives of the north-west coast of America, without the jurisdiction of other nations, are rights which constituted a part of their independence as soon as they declared it. They are rights founded in the law of nations enjoyed in common with all other independent sovereignties, and incapable of being abridged or extinguished,

Case of the "Loriot."

except with their own consent. It is unknown to the Undersigned that they have voluntarily conceded these rights, or either of them, at any time, through the agency of their Government, by Treaty or other form of obligation, in favour of any community.

* * * *

"There is first a mutual and permanent agreement declaratory of their respective rights, without disturbance or restraint, to navigate and fish in any part of the Pacific Ocean, and to resort to its coasts upon points which may not already have been occupied, in order to trade with the natives. These rights pre-existed in each, and were not fresh liberties resulting from the stipulation. To navigate, to fish, and to coast, as described, were rights of equal certainty, springing from the same source, and attached to the same quality of nationality. Their exercise, however, was subjected to certain restrictions and conditions, to the effect that the citizens and subjects of the contracting sovereignties should not resort to points where establishments existed without obtaining permission; that no future establishments should be formed by one party north, nor by the other party south, of 54° 40′ north latitude; but that, nevertheless, both might, for a term of ten years, without regard to whether an establishment existed or not, without obtaining permission, without any hindrance whatever, frequent the interior seas, gulfs, harbours, and creeks, to fish and trade with the natives. This short analysis leaves, on the question at issue, no room for construction.

* * * *

"The Undersigned submits that in no sense can the fourth Article be understood as implying an acknowledgment, on the part of the United States, of the right of Russia to the possession of the coast above the latitude of 54° 40′ north."

In transmitting the papers relative to the "Loriot" to Congress, the President of the United States observed:—

President Van Buren's Message, December 3, 1838, State Papers, by Hertslet, vol. xxvi, p. 1330.

"The correspondence herewith communicated, will show the grounds upon which we contend that the citizens of the United States have, independent of the provisions of the Convention of 1824, a right to trade with the natives upon the coast in question at unoccupied places, liable, however, it is admitted, to be at any time extinguished by the creation of Russian establishments at such points. This right is denied by the Russian Government, which asserts that, by the operation of the Treaty of 1824, each party agreed to waive the general right to land on the vacant coasts on the respective sides of the degree of latitude referred to, and accepted, in lieu thereof, the mutual privileges mentioned in Article IV. The capital and tonnage employed by our citizens in their trade with the north-west coast of America will, perhaps, on adverting to the official statements of the commerce and navigation of the United States for the last few years, be deemed too inconsiderable in amount to attract much attention; yet the subject may, in other respects, deserve the careful consideration of Congress."

Historical outline continued.		To return again to the chronological order of events:—
1837.	North-west Coast, vol. i, p. 342.	In 1837, one foreign trading-vessel is named as having been on the north-west coast.
1838.	Alaska, pp. 552, 553.	In 1838, further explorations were undertaken in the north by Chernof and Malakhof. Three foreign trading-vessels are noted as having been
	North-west Coast, vol. i, p. 342.	on the north-west coast in this year, and one is known to have visited Alaskan waters.
1839.	Alaska, pp. 556, 557	In 1839, a Commission met in London to arrange the dispute between the Hudson's Bay and Russian-American Companies, arising out of the interference by Russian officials with the British vessel "Dryad." The claim for damages by the former Company was waived, on condition that the latter should grant a lease of all their continental territory northward to Cape Spencer, Cross Sound (about latitude 58°), on a fixed rental. This arrangement was for ten years, but was renewed and actually continued in force for twenty-eight years.
1840.	Ibid., p. 557.	In 1840, the British flag was hoisted and saluted at the mouth of the Stikine, the Hudson's Bay Company taking possession. A post was also established by the Company at Taku Inlet.
	Ibid., p. 583, Tiklmenieff. See Appendix, vol. i, No. 5.	At this time whalers were just beginning to resort to Behring Sea; from 1840 to 1842 a large part of the fleet was engaged in whaling on the "Kadiak grounds." Writing in 1842, Etholen says, that for some time he had been constantly receiving reports from various parts of the Colony of the appearance of American whalers in the neighbourhood of the shores.
	Alaska, p. 559.	In the same year Etholen relieved Kuprianof as Governor at Sitka.
1841.	Ibid., p. 568.	In 1841, the Charter of the Russian-American Company was renewed for a further term of twenty years. Etholen reported the presence of fifty foreign whalers in Behring Sea.
1842.	Ibid., p. 583.	In 1842, according to Etholen, thirty foreign whalers were in Behring Sea. He asks the Russian Government to send cruizers to preserve this sea as a *mare clausum*.

His efforts were, however, unsuccessful, the

Minister for Foreign Affairs replying that the Treaty between Russia and the United States gave to American citizens the right to engage in fishing over the whole extent of the Pacific Ocean.

In the same year, inland explorations by Zagoskin, which continued till 1844, began. Sir George Simpson, Governor of the Hudson's Bay Company, reached the Stikine post just in time to prevent an Indian uprising. He also visited the Russian Establishment at Sitka and completed an arrangement between the Companies to interdict trade in spirits on the coast. Alaska, pp. 553, 554.
Ibid., pp. 558-560.

About this time the Russian-American Company became alarmed at the danger to their fur trade. Every effort was, therefore, put forward by the Company and the Governors to induce the Foreign Office of the Russian Government to drive off these whalers from the coasts, and by excluding them for a great distance from shore prevent trespasses on shore and the traffic in furs.

In 1843, explorations were carried out by the Russians on the Snstchina and Copper Rivers. Ibid., p. 576.   1843.

The whalers, from 1843 to 1850, landed on the Aleutian and Kurile Islands, committing depredations. United States' captains openly carried on a traffic in furs with the natives. Ibid., pp. 583, 584.

Tikhmenioff writes :—

"From 1843 to 1850 there were constant complaints by the Company of the increasing boldness of the whalers." Tikhmenieff. See Appendix, vol. i, No. 5.

In 1846 the Governor-General of Eastern Siberia asked that foreign whalers should not be allowed to come within 40 Italian miles of the Russian shores. 1846.

Tikhmenieff thus describes the result of these representations :—

"The exact words of the letter from the Foreign Office are as follows :—

"'The fixing of a line at sea within which foreign vessels should be prohibited from whaling off our shores would not be in accordance with the spirit of the Convention of 1824, and would be contrary to the provisions of our Convention of 1825 with Great Britain. Moreover the adoption of such a measure, without preliminary negotiation and arrangement with the other powers, might lead to protests, since no clear and uniform agreement has yet been arrived at among nations in regard to the limit of jurisdiction at sea.'

"In 1847 a representation from Governor Tebenkof in regard to new aggressions on the part of the whalers gave rise to further correspondence. Some time before, in June 1846, the Governor-General of Eastern Siberia had expressed his opinion that, in order to limit the whaling operations of foreigners, it would be fair to forbid them to come within 40 Italian miles of our shores, the ports of Petropaulovsk and Okhotsk to be excluded, and a payment of 100 silver roubles to be demanded at those ports from every vessel for the right of whaling. He recommended that a ship of war should be employed as a cruizer to watch foreign vessels. The Foreign Office expressly stated as follows, in reply:—

"'We have no right to exclude foreign ships from that part of the Great Ocean which separates the eastern shore of Siberia from the north-western shore of America, or to make the payment of a sum of money a condition to allowing them to take whales.'

"The Foreign Office were of opinion that the fixing of the line referred to above would reopen the discussions formerly carried on between England and France on the subject. The limit of a canon-shot, that is about 3 Italian miles, would alone give rise to no dispute. The Foreign Office observed, in conclusion, that no Power had yet succeeded in limiting the freedom of fishing in open seas, and that such pretentions had never been recognized by the other Powers. They were confident that the fitting out of colonial cruizers would put an end to all difficulties; there had not yet been time to test the efficacy of this measure."

1847.	Tikhmenieff. See Appendix, vol. I, No. 5.	In 1847, traffic in fur-seal skins was carried on by a United States' whaler at Behring Island.
1848.		In 1848, foreign whaling vessels entered the Arctic Ocean by way of Behring Straits for the first time.
1849.	Alaska, p. 584.	In 1849, the whaling fleet in the Arctic and northern part of the North Pacific numbered 290 vessels. Two-thirds of these are said to have been United States' vessels, but others were French and English, the latter chiefly from Australasia. A Russian Whaling Company for the North Pacific was formed at Åbo, in Finland, with special privileges. This Company sent out six vessels in all.
1850.	Ibid., p. 572.	In 1850, the British vessels "Herald," "Plover," and "Investigator," all dispatched in search of Sir John Franklin's expedition, met in Kotzebue Sound, after passing through Behring Strait.
	Ibid., p. 584.	In the same year an armed Russian corvette was ordered to cruize in the Pacific, and in this year it is estimated that 300, and in later years

as many as 500 foreign whalers visited the Arctic and neighbouring waters.

Tebenkof's administration came to an end in this year. *Alaska, p. 585.*

In 1851, Nulato, a fort on the Yukon some way inland, was surprised by Indians and the inmates butchered, including Lieutenant Barnard, an English officer of Her Majesty's ship "Enterprise," one of the ships engaged in the expedition in search of Sir John Franklin. The "Enterprise" passed Behring Strait on the 6th May, 1851. The United States' whaling fleet is said to have been as numerous as in 1849. *Ibid., p. 572. "Encyclopædia Britannica," vol. xix, p. 321.* 1851

The interval between the close of Tebenkof's administration and the beginning of that of Voievodsky was filled by the temporary appointment of Rosenburg and Rudakof. *Alaska, p. 586.*

In 1852, buildings at the Hot Springs, near Sitka, were destroyed by the Indians. *Ibid., p. 574.* 1852.

The value of catch of the whaling fleet in the North Pacific in this year is estimated at 14,000,000 dollars. After 1852 the whaling industry gradually decreased. *Ibid., p. 669.*

In 1853, war impending between England and Russia, the Hudson's Bay and Russian-American Companies influenced their respective Governments to prohibit hostilities on the north-west coast of America. *Ibid., p. 570.* 1853.

In the same year the Russian-American Company again specially requested the Government to prohibit whalers from entering Okhotsk Sea, but without success. Instructions were, however, issued to Russian cruizers to prevent whalers from entering bays or gulfs, or from coming within 3 Italian miles of the shores. *Tikhmenieff. See Appendix, vol. i, No. 5.*

Tikhmenieff gives the following details:—

Some time before the Company had written to the Foreign Office (22nd March, 1853):—

"If it is found impracticable entirely to prohibit for a time fishing by foreigners in the Sea of Okhotsk, as an inland sea, would it not, at any rate, be possible officially to prohibit whalers from coming close to our shores and whaling in the bays and among the islands, detaching one of the cruizers of the Kamtchatka flotilla for this service?" *Ibid.*

The instructions to cruizers were approved on the 9th December, 1853. The cruizers were to see that no whalers entered the bays or gulfs, or came within 3 Italian miles of the shores of Russian America (north of 54° 41'), the Peninsula of Kamtchatka, Siberia, the Kadjak Archipelago, the Aleutian Islands, the Pribyloff and Commander Islands, and the others in Behring Sea, the Kuriles, Sakhalin, the Shantar Islands, and the others in the Sea of Okhotsk to the north of 46° 30' north. The cruizers were instructed constantly to keep in view that :—

"Our Government not only does not wish to prohibit or put obstacles in the way of whaling by foreigners in the northern part of the Pacific Ocean, but allows foreigners to take whales in the Sea of Okhotsk, which, as stated in these instructions, *is, from its geographical position, a Russian inland sea.*" (These words are in italics in the original.)

1854.	Alaska, p. 584.	In 1854, 525 foreign whalers were in Behring Sea and its vicinity. In the same year Voievodsky was elected Governor for the Company.
	Ibid., p. 585.	
1855.	Ibid., p. 585.	In 1855, the Åbo Whaling Company went into liquidation.
1856.	Ibid., p. 584.	In 1856, 366 foreign whalers were reported as in Behring Sea and vicinity.
		Bancroft reports that in the year 1857 :—
	Ibid., p. 668.	"Of the 600 or 700 United States' whalers that were fitted out in 1857, at least one-half, including most of the larger vessels, were engaged in the North Pacific . . . including, of course, Behring Sea."
1857.	50th Cong., 2nd Sess. Sen., Ex. Doc. No. 106, p. 251. Seward to Clay, February 24, 1868. See Appendix, vol. ii, Part II, No. 12. See p. 114 of Case.	Captain Manuel Enos, of the United States' barque "Java," stated in 1867 that he had whaled unmolested in the bays of Okhotsk Sea for seventeen years previously.
1859.	Alaska, p. 592.	In 1859, the cession of Alaska to the United States began to be discussed privately.
1860.	Ibid., pp. 578, 579.	In 1860, the Russian-American Company applied for a new Charter for twenty years, to date from the 1st January, 1862, and Reports as to the condition of the Company were called for by the Government.
	Ibid., p. 580.	The Russian population of the American Colonies at this date, apparently including native wives, numbered 784: Creoles, 1,700; native population estimated at over 7,000.

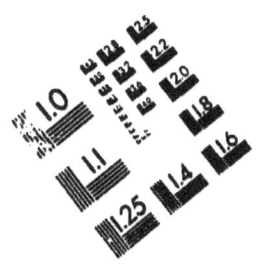 

**IMAGE EVALUATION
TEST TARGET (MT-3)**

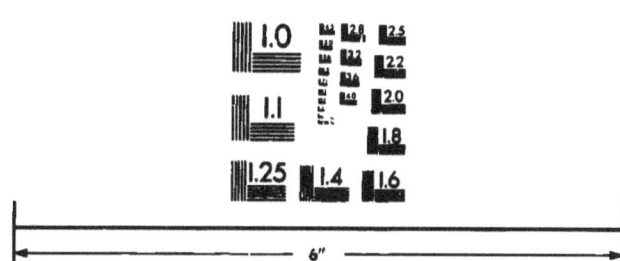

Photographic
Sciences
Corporation

23 WEST MAIN STREET
WEBSTER, N.Y. 14580
(716) 872-4503

In 1862, the value of the catch of the North Pacific whaling fleet was estimated at 800,000 dollars. _{Alaska, p. 669.} 1862.

In 1863, the United States' brig "Timandra" was engaged in the cod fishery off Saghalien Island, Okhotsk Sea. In succeeding years a number of vessels resorted to this sea for the cod fishery. _{Fishery Industries of the United States, sec. v, vol. i, p. 209.} 1863.

In 1864, Maksutof took temporary charge for the Russian Government of the Company's affairs. _{Alaska, p. 570.} 1864.

In 1865, negotiations between the Russian Company and the Government continued, but terms such as the Company would accept could not be arrived at. _{Ibid.} 1865.

In the spring of this year, the "North Pacific cod-fish fleet" was organized. It comprised seven vessels, all of which are believed to have fished in Okhotsk Sea. _{Fishery Industries of the United States, sec. v, vol. i, p. 210.}

In 1866, the Russian Government still contemplated renewing the Company's Charter on certain terms. A Californian Company entered into treaty for a lease of the "coast strip" of Alaska, then held by the Hudson's Bay Company. _{Alaska, p. 580.} 1866.

Eighteen vessels were engaged in the Okhotsk Sea cod fishery. The "Porpoise" initiated the fishery in the Shumagan Group, Alaska, finding there "safe harbours, fuel, water, and other facilities for prosecuting this business." Several British Columbian schooners also fished in Alaskan waters. _{Fishery Industries of the United States, sec. v, vol. i, p. 210.}

In 1867, Alaska was sold by Russia to the United States for 7,200,000 dollars.

Nineteen United States' vessels fished for cod in Okhotsk Sea or in Alaskan waters, the Shumagan fleet consisting of three vessels. The total catch amounted to nearly 1,000,000 fish. _{Ibid., p. 210}

In 1867, before the cession of Alaska, the whaling interest of the United States in these seas are thus referred to by a Philadelphia paper:— _{"Philadelphia North American Gazette," Friday, April 12, 1867. Ex. Doc. No. 177, 2nd Sess., 40th Cong., p. 30.} 1867.

"Our whaling interests are now heaviest in the seas adjacent to Russian-America, both above and below Behring Strait."

The value of the catch of the North Pacific whaling fleet was estimated at 3,200,000 dollars. _{Alaska, p. 660.}

In 1868, the lease of the "coast strip" of Alaska to the Hudson's Bay Company by the Russian-American Company expired. _{Ibid., p. 593.} 1868.

Whaling industry. Statistics of United States' Whaling Industry.

(North Pacific Grounds, including Okhotsk and Behring Seas and Arctic Ocean.)

"Fishery Industries of the United States," sec. 5, vol. ii, pp. 84, 85.

The growth and decline of the whaling industry during the years discussed in this chapter may be conveniently illustrated by the following Table, which shows the number of United States' vessels in the North Pacific whaling fleet from 1841 to 1867. It is taken from "The Fishery Industries of the United States," 1887, section 5, vol. ii, pp. 84-85.

(This list does not include whalers of other nationalities.)

Year.	Number of Vessels.
1841	20
1842	29
1843	108
1844	170
1845	263
1846	292
1847	177
1848	159
1849	155
1850	144
1851	138
1852	278
1853	238
1854	232
1855	217
1856	178
1857	143
1858	196
1859	176
1860	121
1861	76
1862	52
1863	42
1864	68
1865	59
1866	95
1867	90

Walrus hunting.

Ibid, p. 314.

The whaling-vessels frequenting Behring Sea and the Arctic Ocean, from the first, engaged to a certain extent in walrus hunting, and about 1860 such hunting began to be an important secondary object with the whalers. In subsequent years many thousand barrels of walrus oil and great quantities of skins and ivory were secured.

The facts stated in this chapter establish:—

That from the year 1821 to the year 1867 the rights of navigation and fishing in the waters of Behring Sea were freely exercised by the vessels of the United States, Great Britain, and other foreign nations, and were recognized as existing by Russia.

That the waters of Behring Sea were treated by Russia as being subject to the provisions of the Treaties of 1824 and 1825.

CHAPTER V.

The Cession of 1867 and what passed by it.

Cession of 1867 and what passed by it to the United States.

The fourth question or point in Article VI of the Treaty is as follows:—

Did not all the rights of Russia as to jurisdiction and as to the seal fisheries in Behring Sea east of the water boundary, in the Treaty between the United States and Russia of the 30th March, 1867, pass unimpaired to the United States under that Treaty?

This question may conveniently be treated under the following heads, as proposed on p. 10:—

(E.) What rights passed to the United States under the Treaty of the 30th March, 1867.

(F.) The Action of the United States and Russia from 1867 to 1886.

(G.) The contentions of the United States since the year 1886.

HEAD (E).—*What rights passed to the United States under the Treaty of March 30, 1867?*

Text of Treaty of Cession, 1867.

The following is the text of the Treaty of Cession of Alaska as signed:—

United States' Statutes at Large, pp. 539-543. For English version, see Appendix, vol. ii, Part III, No. 3.

"Sa Majesté l'Empereur de Toutes les Russies et les États-Unis d'Amérique, désirant raffermir, s'il est possible, la bonne intelligence qui existe entre eux, ont nommé, à cet effet, pour leurs plénipotentiaires, savoir:

"Sa Majesté l'Empereur de Toutes les Russies, le Conseiller Privé Édouard de Stoeckl, son Envoyé Extraordinaire et Ministre Plénipotentiaire aux États-Unis; et

"Le Président des États-Unis le Sieur William H. Seward, Secrétaire d'État;

"Lesquels, après avoir échangé leurs pleins pouvoirs, trouvés en bonne et due forme, ont arrêté et signé les articles suivants:—

"ARTICLE I.

Treaty of 1867.

"Sa Majesté l'Empereur de Toutes les Russies s'engage par cette convention, à céder aux États-Unis, immédiatement après l'échange des ratifications, tout le territoire avec droit de souveraineté actuellement possédé par Sa Majesté sur le continent d'Amérique, ainsi que les îles contiguës, le dit territoire étant compris dans les limites géographiques ci-dessous indiquées, savoir: la limite orientale est la ligne de démarcation entre les possessions russes et britanniques dans l'Amérique du Nord, ainsi qu'elle est établie par la convention conclue entre la Russie et la Grande-Bretagne, le 16 (28) Février, 1825, et définie dans les termes suivants des articles III et IV. de la dite convention:—

"'A partir du point le plus méridional de l'île dite Prince of Wales, lequel point se trouve sous le parallèle du 54° 40' de latitude nord, et entre le 131ᵐᵉ et le 133ᵐᵉ degré de longitude ouest (méridien de Greenwich), la dite ligne remontera au nord le long de la passe dite Portland Channel, jusqu'au point de la terre ferme, où elle atteint le 56ᵐᵉ degré de latitude nord ; de ce dernier point, la ligne de démarcation suivra la crête des montagnes situées parallèlement à la côte, jusqu'au point d'intersection du 141ᵐᵉ degré de longitude ouest (même méridien) ; et finalement, du dit point d'intersection, la même ligne méridienne du 141 degré formera, dans son prolongement jusqu'à la Mer Glaciale, la limite entre les possessions russes et britanniques sur le continent de l'Amérique nord-ouest.

"'Il est entendu, par rapport à la ligne de démarcation déterminée dans l'article précédent :

"'1°. Que l'île dite Prince of Wales appartiendra toute entière à la Russie' (mais dès ce jour, en vertu de cette cession, aux États-Unis).

"'2°. Que, partout où la crête des montagnes qui s'étendent dans une direction parallèle à la côte, depuis le 56ᵐᵉ degré de latitude nord au point d'intersection du 141ᵐᵉ degré de longitude ouest, se trouverait à la distance de plus de 10 lieues marines de l'océan, la limite entre les possessions britanniques et la lisière de côte mentionnée ci-dessus comme devant appartenir à la Russie' (c'est-à-dire, la limite des possessions cédées par cette convention) : 'sera formée par une ligne parallèle aux sinuosités de la côte et qui ne pourra jamais en être éloignée que de 10 lieues marines.'

"La limite occidentale des territoires cédés passe par un point au Détroit de Behring sous le parallèle du soixante-cinquième degré trente minutes de latitude nord, à son intersection par le méridien qui sépare à distance égale les îles Krusenstern ou Ignalook et l'île Ratmanoff ou Noonarbook, et remonte en ligne directe, sans limitation, vers le nord, jusqu'à ce qu'elle se perde dans la Mer Glaciale. Commençant au même point de départ, cette limite occidentale suit de là un cours presque sud-ouest, à travers le Détroit de Behring et la Mer de Behring, de manière à passer à distance égale entre le point nord-ouest de l'Ile Saint-Laurent et le point sud-est du Cap Choukotski jusqu'au méridien cent soixante-douzième de longitude ouest; de ce point, à partir de l'intersection de ce méridien, cette limite suit une direction sud-ouest de manière à passer à distance égale entre l'Ile d'Attou et l'Ile Copper du groupe d'Ilots Kormandorski dans l'Océan Pacifique Septentrional, jusqu'au méridien de cent quatre-vingt-treize degrés de longitude ouest, de manière à enclaver, dans le territoire cédé, toutes les Iles Aléoutes situées à l'est de ce méridien.

"ARTICLE II.

"Dans le territoire cédé par l'article précédent à la Souveraineté des États-Unis, sont compris le droit de propriété sur tous les terrains et places publics, terres inoccupées, toutes les constructions publiques, fortifications, casernes, et autres édifices qui ne sont pas propriété privée individuelle. Il est, toutefois, entendu et convenu que les églises, construites par le gouvernement russe sur le territoire cédé, resteront la propriété des membres de l'Église Grecque Orientale résidant dans ce territoire et appartenant à ce culte. Tous les archives, papiers, et documents du gouvernement, ayant trait au susdit territoire, et qui y sont maintenant déposés, seront placés entre les mains de l'agent des États-Unis; mais les États-Unis fourniront toujours, quand il y aura lieu, des copies légalisées de ces documents au gouvernement russe, aux officiers ou sujets russes qui pourront en faire la demande.

"ARTICLE III.

"Il est réservé aux habitants du territoire cédé le choix de garder leur nationalité et de rentrer en Russie dans l'espace de trois ans; mais s'ils préfèrent rester dans le territoire cédé, ils seront admis, à l'exception toutefois des tribus sauvages, à jouir de tous les droits, avantages, et immunités des citoyens des États-Unis, et ils seront maintenus et protégés dans le plein exercice de leur liberté, droit de propriété, et religion. Les tribus sauvages seront assujetties aux lois et règlements que les États-Unis pourront adopter, de temps en temps, à l'égard des tribus aborigènes de ce pays.

"ARTICLE IV.

"Sa Majesté l'Empereur de Toutes les Russies nommera, aussitôt que possible, un agent ou aux agents chargés de remettre, formellement, à l'agent ou des agents nommés par les États-Unis, le territoire, la souveraineté, les propriétés, dépendances, et appartenances ainsi cédées et de dresser tout autre acte qui sera nécessaire à l'accomplissement de cette transaction. Mais la cession, avec le droit de possession immédiate, doit toutefois être considérée complète et absolue à l'échange des ratifications, sans attendre la remise formelle.

"ARTICLE V.

"Immédiatement après l'échange des ratifications de cette convention, les fortifications et les postes militaires qui se trouveront sur le territoire cédé seront remis à l'agent des États-Unis, et les troupes russes qui sont stationnées dans le dit territoire seront retirées dans un terme praticable, et qui puisse convenir aux deux parties.

"ARTICLE VI.

"En considération de la susdite cession, les États-Unis s'engagent à payer à la trésorerie à Washington, dans le terme de dix mois après l'échange des ratifications de cette convention, sept millions deux cent mille dollars en or, au représentant diplomatique ou tout autre agent de Sa Majesté l'Empereur de Toutes les Russies dûment autorisé à recevoir cette somme. La cession du territoire avec droit de souveraineté faite par cette convention, est déclarée libre et dégagée de toutes réservations, privilèges, franchises, ou possessions par des compagnies russes ou tout autre, légalement constituées ou autrement, ou par des associations, sauf simplement les propriétaires possédant des biens privés individuels, et la cession ainsi faite transfère tous les droits, franchises, et privilèges appartenant actuellement à la Russie dans le dit territoire et ses dépendances.

"ARTICLE VII.

"Lorsque cette convention aura été dûment ratifiée par Sa Majesté l'Empereur de Toutes les Russies d'une part, et par le Président des États-Unis, avec l'avis et le consentement du sénat, de l'autre, les ratifications en seront échangées à Washington dans le terme de trois mois, à compter du jour de la signature, ou plus tôt si faire se peut.

"En foi de quoi, les plénipotentiaires respectifs ont signé cette convention et y ont apposé le sceau de leurs armes.

"Fait à Washington, le 18 (30) jour de Mars, de l'an de Notre Seigneur mille huit cent soixante-sept.

  (L.S.)   "ÉDOUARD DE STOECKL.
  (L.S.)   "WILLIAM H. SEWARD."

The Treaty discussed.

It may be remarked, in the first place, that though the expression "water boundary" in the question at the head of this chapter may be accepted as an approximate paraphrase of the original expression employed in the Treaty, it is not a correct translation of the words "la limite occidentale des territoires cédés," which are rendered in the official English translation, published by the United States' Government, "the western limit within which the territories and dominion conveyed are contained."

United States' Statutes at Large, vol. xv, 1869, pp. 539–543.

No special dominion over waters

It will be observed that in none of these Articles is there a reference to any extraordinary or special dominion over the waters of the Behring Sea, nor, indeed, over any other portion of the North Pacific Ocean. Even in the passage last cited the word "dominion" appears to have no equivalent in the original French version. Neither is there a suggestion that any special maritime right existed which could be conveyed. The language of the Convention is, on the contrary, most carefully confined to *territory* with the right of sovereignty actually possessed by Russia at the date of the cession.

In Article I the limits of a portion of the Behring Sea are defined in order to show the boundaries within which the territory ceded " sur le Continent d'Amérique ainsi que les îles contiguës" is contained.

In Article VI, Russia again makes it emphatic that she is conveying " ies droits, franchises, et privilèges appartenant actuellement à la Russie dans le dit Territoire et ses dépendances."

The final clause of Article I distinctly negatives any implication of an attempt to convey any portion of the high seas—for the said western line is drawn, not so as to embrace any part of the high seas, but, as expressed in the apt language of the Treaty - " *de manière à enclaver, dans le dit territoire cédé, toutes les Iles Aléou!es situées à l'est de ce méri lien.*"

Had the intention been to convey the waters of the Behring Sea eastward of the western limit, the words "ainsi que les iles contiguës" would not have been used, but words would have been chosen to indicate the area of the open sea conveyed, and it would have been unnecessary to specifically mention the islands.

Character of the western geographical limit, and *reason* for its adoption. Aleutian Islands, &c.

There was good reason for a line of demarcation of the character specified.

The islands in the Aleutian chain and in Behring Sea were not well defined geographically, and could therefore not be used for the accurate delimitation of territory ceded.

In fact, even the term Aleutian Archipelago was indefinite in its signification, often including islands which were on the Asiatic side of Behring Sea, and far from the Island of Attu, the westernmost island of the Aleutian group intended to be ceded.

[218]   O

Greenhow, for instance, writes:—

"The *Aleutian Archipelago* is considered by the Russians as consisting of *three groups* of Islands. Nearest Aliaska are the *Fox Islands*, of which the largest are *Unimak*, *Unalashka*, and *Umnak*; next to these are the *Andreanowsky Islands*, among which are *Atscha*, *Tanaga*, and *Kanaga*, with many smaller islands, sometimes called the *Rat Islands*; the most western group is that first called the *Aleutian* or *Alcoutsky Islands*, which are *Attu*, *Mednoi* (or *Copper Island*), and *Beering's Island*" (p. 5).

Character of the western geographical limit, and reason for its adoption. Aleutian Islands, &c.

"Memoir, Historical and Political, of the North-west Coast of North America, &c., by Robert Greenhow, Translator and Librarian to the Department of State," Senate, 26th Cong., 1st Sess. [174]. 1840.

In the "History of Oregon and California," &c., by the same author, the Commander Islands (Copper and Behring Islands) are again classed among the Aleutian Islands, which are said to be included under two governmental districts by the Russians, the Commander Islands belonging to the western of these districts (p. 38). Greenhow also states that the name "Aleutian Islands" was first applied to Copper and Behring Islands.

Indeed, in many Maps of various dates, the title Aleutian Islands is so placed as implicitly to include the Commander Islands, in some it is restricted to a portion of the chain now recognized by that name. Similar diversity in usage, with frequent instances of the inclusion of the Commander Islands as a part of the Aleutian Islands, is found in geographical works of various dates.

From this uncertainty in usage in respect to the name of the Aleutian Islands (though these are now commonly considered to end to the westward at Attu Island), it is obvious that, in defining a general boundary between the Russian and United States' possessions, it might have given rise to grave subsequent doubts and questions to have stated merely that the whole of the Aleutian Islands belonged to the United States. Neither would this have covered the case presented by the various scattered islands to the north of the Aleutian chain proper, while to have enumerated the various islands, which often appeared and still sometimes appear on different Maps under alternative names, would have been perplexing and unsatisfactory, from the very great number of these to be found in and about Behring Sea.

It was thus entirely natural to define conventionally a general division fixed by an imaginary line so drawn as according to the best published Maps to avoid touching any known islands.

Imperfect survey of Behring Sea.

The occasion for a western limit of the kind adopted is the more obvious, when it is borne in mind that many of the islands in and about Behring Sea are even at the present day very imperfectly surveyed, and more or less uncertain in position.

Appendix No. 2 of United States' Coast Survey. Coast Pilot of Alaska, 1869. Part I, p. 203.

The following is from the "Coast Pilot of Alaska" (United States' Coast Survey, 1869):—

"The following list of the geographical positions of places, principally upon the coast of Alaska, has been compiled chiefly from Russian authorities. In its preparation the intention was to introduce all determinations of position that appeared to have been made by actual observation, even when the localities are quite close. In the Archipelago Alexander most of Vancouver's latitudes have been introduced, although in such waters they are not of great practical value.

"It is believed the latitudes are generally within 2 miles of the actual position, and in many cases where several observers had determined them independently, the errors may be less than a mile. The longitudes of harbours regularly visited by vessels of the Russian-American Company appear to be fairly determined, except toward the western termination of the Aleutian chain, where large discrepancies, reaching 30′ of arc, are exhibited by the comparison of results between Russian authorities and the United States' Exploring Expedition to the North Pacific in 1855. Positions by different authorities are given in some instances to show these discrepancies. The comparison of latitudes and longitudes at Victoria, Fort Simpson, Sitka, Chilkaht, Kadiak, and Unalaska, between English and Russian and the United States' coast survey determinations, exhibit larger errors than might have been expected.

"The uncertainties that exist in the geographical position of many islands, headlands, straits, and reefs, the great dissimilarity of outline and extent of recent examinations of some of the Western Aleutians, the want of reliable data concerning the tides, currents, and winds, the almost total want of detailed descriptions of headlands, reefs, bays, straits, &c., and the circumstantial testimony of the Aleutian fishermen concerning islands visited by them and not laid down upon the Charts, point to the great necessity for an exhaustive geographical reconnaissance of the coast, as was done for the coast of the United States between Mexico and British Columbia."

Even the latest United States' Chart of what are now known as the Aleutian Islands (No. 68, published in 1891) is based chiefly on information obtained by the "North Pacific Surveying Expedition" under Rogers, which was carried out in the schooner "Fenimore Cooper" in 1855. On sheet 1 of this Chart (embracing the western part of the Aleutian

Islands) such notes as the following are found:—

"The latest Russian Charts place Bouldyr Island 10 miles due south of the position given here, which is from a determination by Sumner's method.

"The low islands between Gorcloi and Ioulakh, excepting the west point of Unalga, are from Russian authorities, which, however, are widely discrepant."

Similarly, in the corresponding British Admiralty Chart (No. 1501), published in 1890, we find the remark:—

"Mostly from old and imperfect British, Russian, and American surveys."

On the Chart of Behring Sea, published by the United States in 1891, a small islet is shown north of St. Matthew Island, near the centre of the sea, which does not appear on the special Map of St. Matthew Island published in 1875, and which could not be found in 1891.

That the line drawn through Behring Sea between Russian and United States' possessions was thus intended and regarded merely as a ready and definite mode of indicating which of the numerous islands in a partially explored sea should belong to either Power, is further shown by a consideration of the northern portion of the same line, which is the portion first defined in the Treaty. From the initial point in Behring Strait, which is carefully described, the "limite occidentale" of territories ceded to the United States "remonte en ligne directe, sans limitation, vers le nord, jusqu'à ce qu'elle se perd dans la Mer Glaciale," or, in the United States' official translation "proceeds due north without limitation into the same Frozen Ocean."

The "geographical limit" in this the northern part of its length runs through an *ocean* which had at no time been surrounded by Russian territory, and which had never been claimed as reserved by Russia in any way; to which, on the contrary, special stipulations for access had been made in connection with the Anglo-Russian Convention of 1825, and which since 1848 or 1849 had been frequented by whalers and walrus-hunters of various nations, while no single fur-seal has ever been found within it. It is therefore very clear that the geographical limit thus projected towards the north could have

Limit continued through Arctic

been intended only to define the ownership of such islands, if any, as might subsequently be discovered in this imperfectly explored ocean; and when, therefore, the Treaty proceeded to define the course of "*the same western limit*" (*cette limite occidentale*) from the initial point in Behring Strait to the southward and westward across Behring Sea, it is obvious that it continued to possess the same character and value.

Debates in Congress on the Cession of Alaska,
1867, 1868.

Neither the Debates in Congress—which preceded and resulted in the cession and its ratification by the United States, nor the Treaty by which it was carried into effect, nor the subsequent legislation by the United States, indicate the transfer or acquisition of any exclusive or extraordinary rights in Behring Sea. On the contrary, they show that no such idea was then conceived.

In answer to a Resolution of the House of Representatives of the 10th December, 1867, calling for all correspondence and information in the possession of the Executive in regard to the country proposed to be ceded by the Treaty, the Memorial of the Legislature of Washington Territory (which was made the occasion for the negotiation), together with Mr. Sumner's speech in the Senate, were among other documents transmitted.

This Memorial shows that United States' citizens were already engaged in fishing from Cortez Banks to Behring Strait, and that they had never been under any apprehension of interference with such fishing by Russia, but desired to secure coast facilities, especially for the purposes of curing fish and repairing vessels.

The Memorial is as follows:—

"To his Excellency Andrew Johnson, President of the United States.

"Your memorialists, the Legislative Assembly of Washington Territory, beg leave to show that abundance of codfish, halibut, and salmon, of excellent quality, have been found along the shores of the Russian possessions. Your memorialists respectfully request your excellency to obtain such rights and privileges of the Government of Russia as will enable our fishing-vessels to visit the ports

Marginalia:
Debates in Congress on Cession of Alaska.

Memorial of Legislature of Territory of Washington.

United States' Senate, Ex. Doc. No. 177, 40th Cong., 2nd Sess., p. 132.

and harbours of its possessions to the end that fuel, water, and provisions may be easily obtained; that our sick and disabled fishermen may obtain sanitary assistance, together with the privilege of curing fish and repairing vessels in need of repairs. Your memorialists further request that the Treasury Department be instructed to forward to the Collector of Customs of this Puget Sound district such fishing licences, abstract journals, and log-books as will enable our hardy fishermen to obtain the bounties now provided and paid to the fishermen in the Atlantic States. Your memorialists finally pray your Excellency to employ such ships as may be spared from the Pacific naval fleet in exploring and surveying the fishing banks known to navigators to exist along the Pacific Coast from the Cortez bank to Behring Straits.

" And, as in duty bound, your memorialists will ever pray.

" Passed the House of Representatives, January 10, 1866.

  (Signed) " EDWARD ELDRIDGE, *Speaker*,
        " *House of Representatives.*

" Passed the Council, January 13, 1866.
    "HARVEY K. HINES, *President*
    " *of the Council.*"

In the debate which took place in Congress upon the subject of the acquisition of Alaska, the value of the proposed purchase, and the nature of the interests and property proposed to be acquired, were fully discussed.

The debate was protracted, and many leading Members spoke at length. To none of them did it occur to suggest the existence of an exclusive jurisdiction over any waters or fisheries distant more than 3 miles from land.

On the contrary, Mr. Sumner, who had charge of the measure in the Senate, after pointing out that seals were to be found on the "rocks and recesses" of the territory to be acquired, which would therefore make the acquisition more valuable, in touching upon the fisheries and marine animals found at sea, admitted that they were free to the world, contending, however, that the possession of the coast would give advantages to the United States' fishermen for the outfitting of their vessels and the curing of their catch.

With reference to the whale fishery he remarked:—

Debates in Congress.

" The Narwhal with his two long tusks of ivory, out of which was made the famous throne of the early Danish kings, belongs to the Frozen Ocean; but he, too, strays into the straits below. As no sea is now *mare clausum*, all these may be pursued by a ship under any flag, except directly on the coast and within its territorial

United States' Senate, Ex. Doc. No. 177, 40th Cong., 2nd Sess., p. 183.
See Appendix, vol. i, No. 6.

limit. And yet it seems as if the possession of this coast as a commercial base must necessarily give to its people peculiar advantages in this pursuit."

Mr. Washburn, of Wisconsin, said:—

> United States' Congressional Debates, from "Congressional Globe," December 11, 1867, 40th Cong., 2nd Sess., Part I, p. 135.

"But, Sir, there has never been a day since Vitus Behring sighted that coast until the present when the people of all nations have not been allowed to fish there, and to cure fish so far as they can be cured in a country where they have only from forty-five to sixty pleasant days in the whole year. England, whose relations with Russia are far less friendly than ours, has a treaty with that Government by which British subjects are allowed to fish and cure fish on that coast. Nay, more, she has a treaty giving her subjects for ever the free navigation of the rivers of Russian America, and making Sitka a free port to the commerce of Great Britain."

In 1868 Mr. Ferriss spoke as follows:—

> United States' Congressional Debates, from "Congressional Globe," July 1, 1868, 40th Cong., 2nd Sess., Part IV, p. 3667.

"That extensive fishing banks exist in these northern seas is quite certain; but what exclusive title do we get to them? They are said to be far out at sea, and nowhere within 3 marine leagues of the islands or main shore."

Mr. Peters, in the course of his speech, remarked:—

> Ibid., p. 3668.

"I believe that all the evidence upon the subject proves the proposition of Alaska's worthlessness to be true. Of course, I would not deny that her cod fisheries, if she has them, would be somewhat valuable; but it seems doubtful if fish can find sun enough to be cured on her shores, and if even that is so, my friend from Wisconsin (Mr. Washburn) shows pretty conclusively that in existing treaties we had that right already."

Mr. Williams, in speaking of the value of the fisheries, said:—

> United States' Congressional Debates, from Appendix to "Congressional Globe," July 9, 1868, 40th Cong., 2nd Sess., Part V, p. 490.
>
> See also Alaska, p. 670.

"And now as to the fishes, which may be called, I suppose, the *argumentum piscatorium*. . . . . . Or is it the larger tenants of the ocean, the more gigantic game, from the whale, and seal, and walrus, down to the halibut and cod, of which it is intended to open the pursuit to the adventurous fishermen of the Atlantic coast, who are there already in a domain that is free to all? My venerable colleague (Mr. Stevens), who discourses as though he were a true brother of the angle himself, finds the foundations of this great Republic like those of Venice and Genoa among the fishermen. Beautiful as it shows above, like the fabled mermaid—'*desinit in piscem mulier formosa superne*'—it ends, according to him, as does the Alaska argument itself, in nothing but a fish at last. But the resources of the Atlantic are now, he says, exhausted. The Falkland Islands are now only a resting place in our maritime career, and American liberty can no longer live except by giving to its founders a wider range upon a vaster sea. Think of it, he exclaims—I do not quote his precise language—what a burning shame is it not to us that we have not a spot of earth in all that watery domain on which to refit a mast or sail, or dry a net or fish?—forgetting, all the while, that we have the range of those seas without the leave of anybody; that the privilege of landing anywhere was just as readily attainable, if wanted, as that of hunting on the territory by the British; and, above all, that according to the official Report of Captain Howard, no fishing bank has been discovered within the Russian latitudes."

It is therefore established:—

That Russia's rights " as to jurisdiction and as to the seal fisheries in Behring Sea," referred to in Point 4 of Article VI of the Treaty of 1892, were such only as were hers according to international law, by reason of her right to the possession of the shores of Behring Sea and the islands therein.

That the Treaty of Cession does not purport either expressly or by implication to convey any dominion in the waters of Behring Sea, other than in the territorial waters which would pass according to international law and the practice of nations as appurtenant to any territory conveyed.

That no dominion in the waters of Behring Sea other than in territorial waters thereof did, in fact, pass to the United States by the Treaty of 1867.

CHAPTER VI.

HEAD (F).—*The Action of the United States and Russia from 1867 to 1880.*

n of the United States and Russia from 1867 to 1880.

When, in consequence of the cession of Alaska as a whole, the Russians relinquished their sovereignty over the Pribyloff (or "Seal") Islands in 1867, sealers at once landed on the breeding resorts of the fur-seal on these islands. Those who came from the New England States found themselves confronted by competitors from the Sandwich Islands. They proceeded to slaughter seals upon the breeding grounds in the manner which had usually been practised by sealers on grounds where no Regulations were in force.

Increased slaughter of seals.

Elliott,
Census Report,
p. 25.
H. R., Ex. Doc.
No. 3683, 50th
Cong., 2nd Sess.,
pp. 67, 68.
Ibid., p. 70.

In the year 1868, at least 240,000 seals are reported to have been taken, and 87,000 in the following year. In view of this wholesale destruction of seals, the United States' Government decided, in the exercise of their undoubted right of territorial sovereignty, to lease these seal rookeries, and to re-establish by means of the necessary legislation, the lapsed Russian Regulations which had restricted the killing of the fur-seal.

of July 27, 1868. Killing of seals prohibited.

Accordingly, on the 27th July, 1868, an Act passed the Congress of the United States, entitled "An Act to extend the Laws of the United States relating to Customs and Navigation over the territory ceded to the United States by Russia, to establish a Collection District therein, and for other purposes," of which section 6 provides:—

United States'
Statutes at Large,
vol. xv, p. 241.

"That it shall be unlawful for any person or persons to kill any otter, mink, marten, sable, or fur-seal, or other fur-bearing animal within the limits of *said territory, or in the waters thereof.*"

Ibid., p. 348.

On the 3rd March, 1869, a Resolution was passed by the Senate and House of Representatives specially reserving for Government purposes the Islands of St. Paul and St. George, and forbidding any one to land or remain there without permission of the Secretary of the Treasury.

Secretary Boutwell's Report.

41st Cong., 2nd
Sess., Ex. Doc.
No. 109.

Mr. Boutwell's Report, as Secretary of the Treasury, preceded an Act of the 1st July, 1870. This Report discloses no suggestion of jurisdiction at a greater distance than 3 miles from the shoreline. With knowledge of the raids upon the islands and the existence of seal-hunting schooners, Mr. Boutwell dwelt upon the means of protecting the seal islands only. He recommended that the Government of the United States should itself undertake the management of the business of the islands, and should "exclude everybody but its own servants and agents .... and subject vessels that touch there to forfeiture, except when they are driven to seek shelter or for necessary repairs."

On the 1st July, 1870, an Act was passed entitled, "An Act to prevent the extermination of Fur-bearing animals in Alaska," from which the following are extracts:— *(Act of July, 1870. See Blue Book, United States, No. 2. 1890, p. 12. See Appendix, vol. iii.)*

"Be it enacted by the Senate and House of Representatives of the United States of America in Congress assembled, that it shall be unlawful to kill any fur-seal upon the islands of St. Paul and St. George, *or in the waters adjacent thereto*, except during the months of June, July, September, and October in each year; and it shall be unlawful to kill such seals at any time by the use of fire-arms, or use other means tending to drive the seals away from said islands. . . . .

"Section 2. And be it further enacted, that it shall be unlawful to kill any female seal, or any seal less than 1 year old, at any season of the year, except as above provided; and it shall also be unlawful to kill any seal *in the waters adjacent to said islands*, or on the beaches, cliffs, or rocks where they haul up from the sea to remain.

"Section 4. And be it further enacted, that immediately after the passage of this Act, the Secretary of the Treasury shall lease, for the rental mentioned in section 6 of this Act. . . . . . for a term of twenty years, from the 1st day of May 1870, the right to engage in the business of taking fur-seals on the Islands of St. Paul and St. George, and to send a vessel or vessels to said islands for the skins of such seals. *(Seal Islands to be leased.)*

* * * *

"Section 5. And be it further enacted, that . . . any person who shall kill any fur-seal on either of said islands, *or in the waters adjacent thereto* . . . without authority of the lessees thereof . . . . shall be deemed guilty of a misdemeanour."

In the year 1870, a lease was executed on behalf of the United States' Government in favour of the Alaska Commercial Company, as provided for in this Act. It covered the Islands of St. George and St. Paul only. *(Lease of Alaska Commercial Company. See Appendix, vol. i, No. 7.)*

The following instructions from the Treasury Department show that the administration confined the interference of their officers to those seal-hunters only who attempted landing upon the islands:— *(Instructions to United States' o)*

"*Treasury Department,*
"*September* 10, 1870.

H. R., 44th Cong., "The following Executive Order, relating to the importa-
1st Sess., Ex. Doc. tion of arms into the Islands of St. Paul and St. George,
No. 83, p. 30. within the district of Alaska, is published for the information of officers of the Customs:—

"*Executive Mansion, Washington, D.C.,*
"*September* 9, 1870.

"So much of Executive Order of the 4th February, 1870, as prohibits the importation and use of fire-arms and ammunition into and within the Islands of St. Paul and St. George, Alaska, is hereby modified so as to permit the Alaska Commercial Company to take a limited quantity of fire-arms and ammunition to said islands, subject to the direction of the revenue officers there and such regulations as the Secretary of the Treasury may prescribe.

"U. S. GRANT, *President.*

"The instructions issued by this Department in its Circular of the 8th February, 1870, are accordingly modified so as to adjust them to the above Order.

"Revenue officers will, however, see that the privilege granted to the said Company is not abused; that no fire-arms of any kind are ever used by said Company in the killing of seals or other fur-bearing animals, *on or near said islands*, or near the haunts of seals or sea-otters in the district, nor for any purpose whatever, during the months of June, July, August, September, and October of each year, nor after the arrival of seals in the spring or before their departure in the fall, excepting for necessary protection and defence against marauders or public enemies who may unlawfully attempt to land upon the islands. In all other respects, the instructions of the 8th February, 1870, will remain in force.

"WM. A. RICHARDSON
'*Acting Secretary.*

"*Treasury Department, Washington, D.C.,*
"Sir, "*September* 19, 1870.

H. R., 44th Cong., "I inclose herewith a copy of a letter, dated the 17th
1st Sess., Ex. Doc. instant, from N. L. Jeffries, attorney for the Alaska Com-
No. 83, pp. 32–34. mercial Company, reciting that a Notice recently appeared in the 'Alta California' newspaper, published in your city, of the intended sailing of the schooner 'Mary Zephyr' for the Islands of St. Paul and St. George.

"By the 4th Section of the Act of the 1st July, 1870, entitled 'An Act to prevent the Extermination of Fur-bearing Animals in Alaska,' it is provided that the Secretary of the Treasury, immediately after the passage of said Act, shall lease to proper and responsible parties, &c., &c., the right to engage in the business of taking fur-seals on the Islands of St. Paul and St. George, and to send a vessel or vessels to said islands for the skins of such seals, &c.

"This lease has been awarded to the Company above named for the term of twenty years, a copy of which is herewith inclosed; and the request of General Jeffries that an official announcement be made of the award of said lease, and that no vessels except those of the Government and of said Company will be allowed to touch or land at either of said islands, may be complied with, and you will please cause such Notice to be published in one or more of the San Francisco newspapers, at the expense of said Company.

"I am, &c.,
(Signed) "WM. A. RICHARDSON,
"*Acting Secretary.*
"T. G. Phelps, Esq.,
 "Collector of Customs,
  "San Francisco, California.

"*Custom-house, San Francisco, California,*
"Sir, "*Collector's Office, September* 30, 1870.
"I have the honour to acknowledge the receipt of your letter of the 19th instant, relative to the published Notice of the sailing of the schooner 'Mary Zephyr' for the Islands of St. Paul and St. George, in Alaska. On seeing the advertisement in the 'Alta,' written Notice was immediately sent to the parties interested, that no vessel would be permitted to land at said islands. I have caused a Notice, as suggested by the honourable Secretary, to be published. Please find a copy of the Notice inclosed.

"I am, &c.,
(Signed) "T. G. PHELPS,
"*Collector.*
"Honourable Geo. S. Boutwell,
 "Secretary, Treasury.

"*Notice.*

"In compliance with an order of the honourable Secretary of the Treasury, notice is hereby given that a lease of the Islands of St. Paul and St. George, in the Territory of Alaska, has been executed by the Secretary of the Treasury to the Alaska Commercial Company for the period of twenty years from the 1st day of May, 1870, in accordance with the provisions of an Act of Congress entitled 'An Act to prevent the Extermination of Fur-bearing Animals in Alaska,' approved the 1st July, 1870, and that, by the terms of said lease and the above-mentioned Act, the said Company have the exclusive right to engage in the business of taking fur-seals on said islands and the islands adjacent thereto. No vessels, other than those belonging to said Alaska Commercial Company or to the United States, will be permitted to touch or land at either of said islands or the islands adjacent thereto, nor will any person be allowed thereon except the authorized agents of the United States and of said Company.

(Signed) "T. G. PHELPS,
"*Collector of Customs.*
"*Custom-house, San Francisco, California,*
 "*Collector's Office, September* 28, 1870."

...o of United States' Government in 1872 as to jurisdiction.

50th Cong., 2nd Sess., Senate Ex. Doc. No. 106, pp. 139, 140.

When the above-mentioned legislation was enacted, Mr. Boutwell, as already stated, was Secretary of the United States' Treasury. The following correspondence between Mr. T. G. Phelps and Mr. Boutwell shows the position assumed in 1872 by the Treasury Department in relation to the extent of jurisdiction of the United States in Alaskan waters:—

"*Mr. Phelps to Mr. Boutwell.*

"*Customs House, San Francisco,
Collector's Office, March 25, 1872.*

"Sir.

"I deem it proper to call the attention of the Department to certain rumours which appear to be well authenticated, the substance of which appears in the printed slip taken from the 'Daily Chronicle' of this date, herewith inclosed.

"In addition to the several schemes mentioned in this paper, information has come to this office of another which is being organized at the Hawaiian Islands for the same purpose. It is well known that, during the month of May and the early part of June in each year, the fur-seal, in their migration from the southward to St. Paul and St. George Islands, uniformly move through Oonimak Pass in large numbers, and also through the narrow straits near that pass which separate several small islands from the Aleutian group.

"The object of these several expeditions is unquestionably to intercept the fur-seals at these narrow passages during the period above mentioned, and there, by means of small boats manned by skilful Indians or Aleutian hunters, make indiscriminate slaughter of those animals in the water, after the manner of hunting sea-otters.

"The evil to be apprehended from such proceedings is not so much in respect of the loss resulting from the destruction of the seals at those places (although the killing of each female is in effect the destruction of two seals), but the danger lies in diverting these animals from their accustomed course to the islands of St. Paul and St. George, their only haunts in the United States.

"It is believed by those who have made the peculiar nature and habits of these animals a study, that if they are by any means seriously diverted from the line upon which they have been accustomed to move northward in their passage to these islands, there is great danger of their seeking other haunts, and should this occur the natural selection would be Komandorsky Islands, which lie just opposite the Pribylov group, near the coast of Kamschatka, owned by Russia, and are now the haunt of fur-seals.

"That the successful prosecution of the above-mentioned schemes would have the effect to drive the seals from their accustomed course there can be no doubt. Considering, therefore, alone the danger which is here threatened to the interest of the Government in the seal fisheries, and the large annual revenue derived from the same, I have the honour to suggest, for the consideration of the Honourable Secretary of the Treasury, the question whether the Act of July 1, 1870, relating to those fisheries, does not authorize his interference by means of revenue cutters to prevent foreigners and others from doing such an irreparable mischief to this valuable interest. Should the Honourable Secretary deem it expedient to send a cutter into those waters, I would respectfully suggest that a steam-cutter would be able to render the most efficient service, and that it should be in the region of Oonimak Pass and St. Paul and St. George Islands by the 15th of May next.

"I am, &c.
(Signed) "T. G. PHELPS, *Collector.*

[*From San Francisco "Daily Chronicle," March 21, 1872.*]

"It is stated in reliable commercial circles that parties in Australia are preparing to fit out an expedition for the capture of fur-seals in Behring Sea. The present high prices of fur-seal furs in London and the European markets has acted powerfully in stimulating enterprises of a like character. But a few days ago we mentioned that a Victorian Company was organized for catching fur-seals in the North Pacific. Another party—an agent representing some Eastern capitalists—has been in this city for the past week making inquiries as to the feasibility of organizing an expedition for like purposes.

"*Mr. Boutwell to Mr. Phelps.*

"*Treasury Department, Washington, D.C.,*
"Sir, "*April* 19, 1872.

"Your letter of the 25th ultimo was duly received calling the attention of the Department to certain rumours circulating in San Francisco, to the effect that expeditions are to start from Australia and the Hawaiian Islands to take fur-seals on their annual migration to the Islands of St. Paul and St. George through the narrow Pass of Oonimak. You recommend—to cut off the possibility of evil resulting to the interests of the United States from these expeditions—that a revenue cutter be sent to the region of Oonimak Pass by the 15th May next.

"A very full conversation was held with Captain Bryant upon this subject while he was at the Department, and he conceived it to be entirely impracticable to make such an expedition a paying one, inasmuch as the seals go singly or in pairs, and not in droves, and cover a large region of water in their homeward travel to these islands, and he did not seem to fear that the seals would be driven from their accustomed resorts, even were such attempts made.

"In addition, I do not see that the United States would have the jurisdiction or power to drive off parties going up there for that purpose, unless they make such attempt within a marine league of the shore.*

"As at present advised, I do not think it expedient to carry out your suggestions, but I will thank you to communicate to the Department any further facts or information you may be able to gather upon the subject.

"I am, &c.

(Signed) "GEORGE S. BOUTWELL,
Secretary."

1875.

Opinion of Secretary Fish.

44th Cong., 1st Sess., H. R., Ex. Doc. No. 130, p. 124, March 15, 1875.

In 1875 Mr. McIntyre, the Assistant Treasury Agent at the Pribyloff Islands, wrote that he had armed the natives with the intention of repelling by force attempts "to kill seals in the rookeries or within a rifle shot of the shore."

In 1875, a question having arisen as to Russia's authority to grant licences for the use of the seas contiguous to her coasts, Mr. Fish, Secretary of State for the United States of America, gives conclusive evidence as to the interpretation placed upon the Convention of 1824 by the United States, as follows:—

Fish to Boker, Dec. 1, 1875, Wharton, vol i, sec. 32, p. 106.

"There was reason to hope that the practice which formerly prevailed with powerful nations of regarding *seas* and *bays, usually of large extent,* near their coast, *as closed to any foreign commerce or fishery* not specially licensed by them, was, without exception, *a pretension of the past,* and that no nation would claim exemption from the general rule of public law which limits its maritime jurisdiction to a marine league from its coast. We should particularly regret if Russia should insist on any such pretension."

...ig and navigation by foreigners.

H. R., Ex. Doc. No. 35, 44th Cong., 1st Sess.

During the whole period discussed in this chapter, the vessels of various nations were continuously engaged in hunting, fishing, and navigating in the waters of the North Pacific, including Behring Sea.

Schooners from British Columbia were fishing for cod as early as 1860, and seals to the number of 20,000 a-year were reported as being taken south of St. George and St. Paul Islands in 1870 and 1872.

Ex parte S. H. Cooper, owner of "W. P. Sayward." Brief for the United States, No. 9, October Term, 1890, p. 197.

* In 1888 (after the occurrence of the seizures of British vessels in 1886 and 1887) Mr. Boutwell, by request, explained, in a letter dated the 18th January, that 'neither upon my recollection of facts, as they were understood by me in 1872, nor upon the present reading of the correspondence, do I admit the claim of Great Britain that my letter is an admission of any right adverse to the claims of the United States in the waters known as Behring Sea. My letter had reference solely to the waters of the Pacific Ocean south of the Aleutian Islands."

Whalers continued as before to frequent the waters both east and west of the line described in the Treaty of 1867. The extent of their operations appears from the following Table, which shows the number of vessels composing the North Pacific whaling fleet after the date of the Alaska Cession.*

Whaling industry.

Fishery Industries of the United States, 1887, sec. 5, vol. ii, p. 83.

Year.	Number of United States' Vessels.	Remarks.
1867	90	Also eleven foreign vessels.
1868	61	Also seven foreign vessels.
1869	43	Also six foreign vessels.
1870	46	Also nine foreign vessels.
1871	35	All but seven of the fleet were lost, including four foreign vessels.
1872	27	Also four foreign vessels.
1873	30	Also four foreign vessels.
1874	23	Also four foreign vessels.
1875	16	Also four foreign vessels.
1876	18	All but eight of the fleet lost, also two foreign vessels.
1877	19	Three of the fleet were lost; one foreign vessel.
1878	17	One of the fleet lost.
1879	21	Three of the fleet lost.
1880	19	

Walrus hunting is also known to have been continuously practised by the whalers during these years, and in some years large quantities of walrus ivory and oil were obtained:—

Walrus hunting.

Fishery Industries of the United States, sec. 5, vol. ii, part 17, pp. 318 et seq.

"The Arctic whaling fleet from 1870 to 1880, inclusive, is estimated to have captured 100,000 walrus, producing 1,996,000 gallons of oil and 398,868 lbs. of ivory, of a total value of 1,260,000 dollars."

In 1872 expeditions for sealing in Behring Sea were reported to be fitting out in various places, as appears from Mr. Phelps' letter of the 25th March in that year, already quoted, and in 1875 a schooner was reported as having been seen shooting seals among the seal islands.

Seal hunting.

H. R., Ex. Doc. No 83, p. 125, 44th Cong., 1st Sess.

Ivan Petroff, Special Commissioner of the United States to the seal islands in the year 1880, says in his Report:—

"As these seals pass up and down the coast as far as the Straits of Fuca and the mouth of Columbia River, quite a number of them are secured by hunters, who shoot or spear them as they find them asleep at sea. Also, small vessels are fitted out in San Francisco, which regularly cruize in these waters for the purpose alone of shooting sleeping seal."

H. R., Ex Doc. No. 40, 46th Cong., 3rd Sess., vol. xviii, p. 65.

---

* All vessels not sailing under the United States' flag are specified in this Table as "foreign."

And he adds:—

H. R., Ex. Doc. No. 40, 45th Cong., 3rd Sess., vo'. xvii, p. 68.

"The fur trade of this country, with the exception of that *confined to the seal islands* and set apart by law, is free to all legitimate enterprise."

H. R., Ex. Doc. No. 133, 49th Cong., 1st Sess.

Sealing-vessels and their catches were also reported by the United States' cutter "Corwin," but none were interfered with when outside of the 3-mile limit.

H. R., Ex. Doc. No. 3883, 50th Cong., 2nd Sess., p. 58.

In 1881 an Agent of the United States' Government stated that during the past twenty years probably 100 vessels had "prowled" about the Pribyloff Islands.

Complaints of depredations on rookeries.

The Agents of the United States' Government sent to the seal islands previously to 1880 continually reported upon the inadequacy of the protection of the islands, and they frequently referred to depredations upon the rookeries by the crews of vessels sealing in Behring Sea.

Letter from Mr. d'Ancona.

Early in 1881, Collector D. A. d'Ancona, of San Francisco, appears to have requested information from the Treasury Department at Washington in regard to the meaning placed by that Department upon the law regulating the killing of fur-bearing animals in the territory of Alaska, and specially as to the interpretation of the terms "waters thereof" and "waters adjacent thereto," as used in the law, and how far the jurisdiction of the United States was to be understood as extending.

Reply of Mr. French.

In reply, Acting Secretary H. F. French, of the Treasury Department, wrote as follows on the 12th March, 1881:—

"Sir,

H. R., Ex. Doc., 50th Cong., 2nd Sess., No. 3883, p. 281.

"Your letter of the 19th ultimo, requesting certain information in regard to the meaning placed by this Department upon the law regulating the killing of fur-bearing animals in the Territory of Alaska, was duly received. The law prohibits the killing of any fur-bearing animals, except as otherwise therein provided, within the limits of Alaska Territory or in the waters thereof, and also prohibits the killing of any fur-seals on the Islands of St. Paul and St. George or in the waters adjacent thereto, except during certain months.

"You inquire in regard to the interpretation of the terms 'waters thereof' and 'waters adjacent thereto,' as used in the law, and how far the jurisdiction of the United States is to be understood as extending.

"Presuming your inquiry to relate more especially to the waters of Western Alaska, you are informed that the Treaty with Russia of the 30th March, 1870 [*sic*], by which the Territory of Alaska was ceded to the United States, defines the boundary of the Territory so ceded. This Treaty is found on pp. 671 to 673 of the volume of Treaties of the Revised Statutes. It will be seen therefrom that the limit of the cession extends from a line starting from the Arctic Ocean and running through Bering Strait to the north of St. Lawrence Islands. The line runs thence in a south-westerly direction, so as to pass midway between the Island of Attoo and Copper Island of the Kromanhowski [sic] complet or group, in the North Pacific Ocean, to meridian of 193 degrees of west longitude. All the waters within that boundary to the western end of the Aleutian Archipelago and chain of islands, are considered as comprised within the waters of Alaska Territory.

"All the penalties prescribed by law against the killing of fur-bearing animals would therefore attach against any violation of law within the limits before described.

(Signed) "H. F. French,
"Acting Secretary."

It does not appear from any official documents that any action was taken at the time in accordance with the opinion expressed in this letter, and no seizures were made, and no warning was given to any British vessel engaged in sealing beyond the ordinary territorial limits prior to 1886, although at least one British vessel is known to have been engaged in such sealing in 1884, and no less than thirteen were so engaged in 1885. Two of these vessels are stated to have been spoken by a United States' revenue-cutter, without being in any way molested.

On the 22nd May, 1884, Lieutenant I. E. Lutz was instructed by the Captain of the United States' revenue-steamer "Corwin" to watch and to seize or arrest any vessel or persons attempting to take seals contrary to law.

Acting under these instructions, Lieutenant Lutz arrested the "Adèle," of Hamburg, Gustave Isaacson, master, with three officers and a crew of eighteen Japanese, when at anchor off shore. The Lieutenant was careful to ascertain that the vessel was engaged in sealing ashore, and having waited the return of the ship's boat which came back loaded with seal carcasses, Lieutenant Lutz reported that, *having now secured all necessary evidence*, he notified the captain of the seizure of the vessel.

It is found that from 1867 down to and including 1885, vessels continued to visit and hunt in Behring Sea without interference when outside of the ordinary territorial jurisdiction.

The circumstances which appear to have led to a change of official policy in 1886 will be related hereafter.

It may be convenient at this point to refer to questions which were raised by occurrences in the Asiatic waters of the Pacific, adjacent to Russian territory.

No seizures made before 1886.

50th Cong., 2nd Sess., Senate Ex. Doc. No. 106, p. 134.

H. R., Mis. Doc., 50th Cong., 1st Sess., No. 602, p. 28.

Ibid., p. 33.

Questions arising between the United States and Russia in Okhotsk and Behring Seas.

Disputes in Okhotsk and Behring Seas.

Disputes have more than once arisen respecting the rights of United States' whaling-vessels in Okhotsk Sea.

Whalers in Okhotsk Sea.

Fishery Industries of the United States, section 5, vol. ii, p. 20. See extract from Tikhmenieff, Appendix, vol. i, No. 5.

The main objection to these whalers was that they interfered with the fur industry, and it is on record that the mode of whaling practised in this sea was often to anchor the vessel in some harbour and to send the boats therefrom in pursuit of whales. The instructions to Russian cruizers, dating from 1853, only prohibited these vessels from coming " within 3 Italian miles of our shores." The Sea of Okhotsk was covered by the Ukase of 1821, and possesses a seal rookery (Robben Island). Whalers from the United States and elsewhere began to frequent this sea about the year 1843.

Whalers sometimes seal-hunters.

The following evidence with reference to sealing and whaling in Okhotsk Sea given before the Committee of Ways and Means in the House of Representatives at Washington (3rd May, 1876), shows that whalers were also engaged in taking seals:—

H. R., 44th Cong., 1st Sess., Report 623.

"Q. Who are Williams, Haven, and Co.?—A. Williams, Haven, and Co. are Mr. Henry P. Haven, of Connecticut, who died last Sunday, and Richard Chapel. They are whalers. They took seals and whales, and had been at that business in the Pacific for a great many years.

"Q. They had an interest in these skins?—A. Yes, Sir. They had a vessel in the waters of the Okhotsk Sea, I think, seal-fishing in 1866. While their vessel was at Honolulu in 1866, the captain became acquainted with a Russian captain who put in there in distress with the remainder, or a portion, of the Alaska seal-skins taken by the old Russian Company, and there this captain learned of this interest. He left his vessel at Honolulu, went to Connecticut, and conferred with his employers. Then Mr. Chapel, one of the concern, went out to Honolulu and fitted out this vessel and another one and sent them to the Alaska Islands as early as April 1868."

Mr. Hoffman to Mr. Frelinghuysen, March 14, 1882.

The United States' Minister at St. Petersburg, Mr. Hoffman, writing in 1882, thus refers to this sea:—

50th Cong., 2nd Sess., Senate Ex. Doc. No. 106, p. 260. See Appendix, vol. ii, Part II, No. 14.

"A glance at the Map will show that the Kurile Islands are dotted across the entrance to the Sea of Okhotsk the entire distance from Japan on the south to the southernmost Cape of Kamtchatka on the north.

"In the time when Russia owned the whole of these islands, her Representatives in Siberia claimed that the Sea of Okhotsk was a *mare clausum*, for that Russian jurisdiction extended from island to island and over

[248]   Q 2

2 marine leagues of intermediate sea from Japan to Kamtchatka.

"But about five years ago Russia ceded the southern group of these islands to Japan, in return for the half of the Island of Saghalien, which belonged to that Power.

"As soon as this was done it became impossible for the Siberian authorities to maintain their claim. My informant was not aware that this claim had ever been seriously made at St. Petersburg."

And in another letter he says:—

"I do not think that Russia claims that the Sea of Okhotsk is a *mare clausum*, over which she has exclusive jurisdiction. If she does, her claim is not a tenable one since the cession of part of the group of the Kurile Islands to Japan, if it ever were tenable at any time."

March 27, 1882.
50th Cong., 2nd Sess., Senate Ex. Doc. No. 106, p. 261.
See Appendix, vol. ii, Part II, No. 15.

The following appears as an introductory statement in "Papers relating to Behring Sea Fisheries," published at the Government Printing Office in Washington, 1887:—

"This sea [of Okhotsk] is a part of the waters to which the Ukase of 1821 applied, and which M. Poletica, in his subsequent correspondence with Mr. Adams, prior to the Treaty of 1824, said His Imperial Majesty, the Emperor of all the Russias, might have claimed as a close sea had he chosen to do so. As has been seen, all question as to the right of citizens of the United States, as well as of the subjects of Great Britain, to navigate and fish in those waters, was given up by Russia once for all in the Treaty of 1824 with the United States, and of 1825 with Great Britain.

"The following correspondence between Russia and the United States in the years 1867 and 1868 contains an explicit disavowal by Russia of any claim to interfere with the fishing operations of citizens of the United States in the Sea of Okhotsk."

Okhotsk Sea subject to Ukase of 1821.

The correspondence referred to shows that the captain of the "Europa," a United States' whaling-vessel, complained to the Department of State at Washington that the Captain of a Russian armed steamer had stated that he was authorized to drive United States' whalers away from the vicinity of the Settlement of Okhotsk, in the Sea of Okhotsk, and that he had fired on the ship's boat of the bark "Endeavour," of New Bedford.

It appears also from the same correspondence that on the 27th July, 1867, the United States' bark "Java" was cruizing for whales in Shantar Bay and standing towards Silas Richard's Bluff, when a Russian Commander ordered him out of the bay, and thereupon Mr. Seward inquired

Interference with United States' vessels
"Europa."

"Endeavour."

"Java."

Seward to Clay, February 24, 1868, vol. ii, Part II, No. 12.

of the Russian Government what instructions had been issued relating to fisheries in this sea.

Explanations by Russi

Westmann to United States' Secretary of State, July 31, 1868, 50th Cong., 2nd Sess., Senate Ex. Doc. No. 106, p. 233.

In reply to this inquiry, the following explanation was received from M. de Westmann, Acting Minister of Foreign Affairs at St. Petersburg, which shows the claim of jurisdiction of Russia to have been confined to 3 miles only in Russian gulfs and bays, in this part of the very waters covered by the Ukase of 1821:—

claim of jurisdiction beyond 3-mile limit.

"These are the circumstances: The schooner 'Aleout,' under the command of Lieutenant Etoline, had been sent in commission from Nicolaievsk to Oudrk. The abundance of floating ice having forced him to enter into the Gulf of Tougoursh, he there met, the 14th July, at about 20 miles to the south of the Straits of Chautarsk, near the eastern coast, the American whaler 'Java,' occupied in rendering the oil of a captured whale. Considering that foreign whalers are forbidden by the laws in force to fish in the Russian gulfs and bays at a distance of less than 3 miles from the shore, where the right of fishing is exclusively reserved to Russian subjects, Lieutenant Etoline warned (' invita') the captain of the 'Java' to 'bear off' from the Gulf of Tougoursh, which he at once did. The same day the 'Aleout' made for the Bay of Mawgon, where arrived, on the next day, the American whale schooner 'Caroline Foot,' whose captain, accompanied by the captain of the 'Java,' called on Lieutenant Etoline, and declared that he had no right to prevent them from fishing for whales wherever they liked. Lieutenant Etoline replied that there were in that respect established rules ('règles'), and if they insisted, absolutely, upon breaking them, that he would be compelled to prevent them. The captain of the schooner 'Caroline Foot' pretending ('ayant prétendu') that he had entered into the Bay of Tougoursh in consequence of 'deviations from his course,' Lieutenant Etoline offered at once all assistance in his power; and, upon request, delivered him 7 pouds of biscuit from the stores of the 'Aleout,' after which the two ships again went to sea. The 19th of July, that is, four days afterwards, the schooner 'Aleout' met a whale, upon which the Commander caused a trial fire to be made. At the same moment was seen, at about 16 miles distance, a sail, name unknown, and, nearer, three 'chaloupes,' the nearest of which was at least 3 miles in advance in the direction of the cannon fire. In the evening all these ships had disappeared. That incident is registered in the books of the 'Aleout' in the following terms: 'The 19th of July, at 9 in the evening, at anchor in the Bay of Mawgons, fired a cannon shot for practice at a whale afloat.' From these facts General Clay will be convinced that the incident alluded to has been exaggerated, and even perverted ('dénaturé') much in order to be represented as a cause of grievance against the Commander of the 'Aleout' on the part of the American whalers."

The explanation was considered satisfactory, Mr. Seward observing that "the captain of the 'Java,' spoke unwarrantably when by implication he denied that the Russian authorities have the right to prevent foreign vessels from fishing for whales within 3 marine miles of their own shore."

50th Cong., 2nd Sess., Senate Ex. Doc. No. 106, p. 255.

In the year 1881 the Russian Consul at Yokohama issued, on behalf of the Russian Imperial Government, a Notice, of which the following is a translation:—

"NOTICE.

"At the request of the local authorities of Behring and other islands, the Undersigned hereby notifies that the Russian Imperial Government publishes, for general knowledge, the following:

"'1. Without a special permit or licence from the Governor-General of Eastern Siberia, foreign vessels are not allowed to carry on trading, hunting, fishing, &c., on the Russian coast or islands in the Okhotsk and Behring Seas, or on the north-eastern coast of Asia, or within their sea boundary-line.

"'2. For such permits or licences, foreign vessels should apply to Vladivostock exclusively.

"'3. In the port of Petropaulovsk, though being the only port of entry in Kamtchatka, such permits or licences shall not be issued.

"'4. No permits or licences whatever shall be issued for hunting, fishing, or trading at or on the Commodore and Robben Islands.

"'5. Foreign vessels found trading, fishing, hunting, &c., in Russian waters, without a licence or permit from the Governor-General, and also those possessing a licence or permit who may infringe the existing bye-laws on hunting, shall be confiscated, both vessels and cargoes, for the benefit of the Government. This enactment shall be enforced henceforth, commencing with A.D. 1882.

"'6. The enforcement of the above will be intrusted to Russian men-of-war, and also to Russian merchant-vessels, which, for that purpose, will carry military detachments and be provided with proper instructions.

"'A. PELIKAN,
"'H. I. R. M. Consul.
"'Yokohama, November, 15, 1881.'"

Russian Notice of November 1881 r Okhotsk and Behring Seas.

Ibid., p. 259.

The firm of Messrs. Lynde and Hough, of San Francisco, was in 1882, and had been for years, engaged in the Pacific coast fisheries. They yearly sent vessels to the Sea of Okhotsk, fishing from 10 to 20 miles from shore. The attention of the firm being called to the above Notice, they wrote to the Secretary of State of the United States calling attention thereto.

Ibid., p. 259. Lynde and Hough to Folger, February 15, 1882. See Appendix, vol. II, Part II, No. 13.

The Secretary of State (Mr. Frelinghuysen), on the 7th March, 1882, inclosed their letter, together with the Regulations "touching the Pacific coast fisheries," as he termed them, to Mr. Hoffman, the United States' Minister at St. Petersburg. Mr. Hoffman acknowledged the receipt of this despatch, in reference to what he also called "our Pacific Ocean fisheries."

Mr. Hoffman, having made inquiry of M. de Giers, the Russian Foreign Minister, the latter, in his reply, dated the 8th (20th) May, 1882, explained that these Regulations applied only to "territorial waters of Russia," and, in a subsequent letter of the 1st (13th) June, quoted Article 560 of the Russian Code, which is as follows:—

"ARTICLE 560.

"The maritime waters, even when they wash the shores, where there is a permanent population, can not be the subject of private possession; they are open to the use of one and all."

In a letter to Mr. Frelinghuysen of the 14th March, 1882, Mr. Hoffman shows what he understood to be the meaning applied by M. de Giers to the words "territorial waters." He writes:—

"The best whaling grounds are found in *the bays and inlets* of the Sea of Okhotsk. Into these the Russian Government does not permit foreign whalers to enter, *upon the ground that the entrance to them, from headland to headland, is less than 2 marine leagues wide.*"

Indeed, M. de Giers, in the letter of the 8th (20th) May, 1882, already quoted, makes it clear that, as to fishing and hunting, the rule was the same, and that the prohibition of vessels engaged in these pursuits extended only over the marine league from the shores of the coasts "and the islands called the 'Commander' and the 'Seals.'"

The island referred to as the "Seals" is Robben Island, and the reference to this and the Commander Islands indicates that M. de Giers, under the term of "hunting," was referring specially to the sealing industry.

On the 21st July, 1884, the United States' schooner "Eliza" was seized by the Russian cruizer "Razboïnik" in the Anadir River, which runs into Anadir Bay, a northern portion of Behring Sea. It was represented to the United

States that she was there trading and hunting walrus. The United States' Vice-Consul-General at Japan termed the seizure "an act of piracy."

50th Cong., 2nd Sess., Senate Ex Doc. No. 106, p. 263.

General Vlangaly, writing from the Department of Foreign Affairs on the 19th (31st) January, 1887, explained that the "Eliza" was arrested, "not for the fact of seal-hunting," but for violating the prohibition touching trading, hunting, and fishing on the Russian coasts of the Pacific without special licence.

Ibid., p. 270. See Appendix, vol. ii, Part II, No. 19.

The crew, it was found, were trading with the natives on the coasts of Kamtchatka, as well as hunting walrus.

Ibid., p. 269.

This appears to have been accepted as a valid explanation; but with reference to the seizure of this ship and of the "Henrietta," Mr. Lothrop, United States' Minister at St. Petersburg, writing to Mr. Bayard, the United States' Secretary of State, on the 17th February, 1887, remarks:—

Ibid. See Appendix, vol. ii, Part II, No. 19.

"I may add that the Russian Code of Prize Law of 1869, Article 21, and now in force, limits the jurisdictional waters of Russia to 3 miles from the shore."

The United States' schooner "Henrietta" had been seized on the 29th August, 1886, off East Cape in Behring Strait by the Russian corvette "Kreysser."

Case of the "Henrietta."

Ibid., p. 267.

Explanations from the Russian Government were promptly demanded by the United States, and it was alleged she was arrested for illicit trading on the Russian coasts.

Ibid., p. 269. See Appendix, vol. ii, Part II, No. 18.

Nevertheless, Mr. Bayard, writing to Mr. Lothrop on the 16th March, 1887, observed:—

Views of Mr. Bayard.

"If, as I am to conclude from your despatch, the seizure of the 'Henrietta' was made in Russian territorial waters, then the Russian authorities had jurisdiction; and if the condemnation was on proceedings duly instituted and administered before a competent Court and on adequate evidence, this Department has no right to complain. But if either of these conditions does not exist, the condemnation cannot be internationally sustained. The first of these conditions, viz., that the proceedings should have been duly instituted and administered, could not be held to exist if it should appear that the Court before whom the proceedings were had was composed of parties interested in the seizure. On general principles of international law, to enforce a condemnation by such a Court is a denial and perversion of justice, for which this Government is entitled to claim redress.

Papers relating to Behring Sea Fisheries, published at the Government Printing Office in Washington, 1887, p. 121.

"The same right to redress, also, would arise if it should appear that, while the seizure was within the 3-mile zone, the alleged offence was committed exterior to that zone and on the high seas.

"You are therefore instructed to inquire, not merely as to the mode in which the condemning Court was constituted, but as to the evidence adduced before such Court, in which the exact locality of seizure should be included."

o assertion by United States of extra-minary jurisdiction previous to 1886.

The instructions given from time to time to Commanders of the Revenue Service, or of ships of war of the United States cruizing in Behring Sea, and guarding the interests of the Alaska Commercial Company upon the islands leased to the Company, do not even suggest the intention of that Government to assert a claim so vehemently disputed when advanced by Russia.

On the contrary, while vessels from British Columbia and elsewhere were trading and fishing generally in the Behring Sea, and while vessels—chiefly those of the United States—were actually raiding the rookeries, the instructions relating to the fisheries given to Revenue Marine vessels by the United States' Government, until 1886, were confined, as has been shown, to the immediate protection of the seal islands.

ort of cruize of the "Corwin," 1885

The seizure of British sealers in the open sea followed the report on the cruize of the Revenue Marine steamer "Corwin" in the year 1885.

H. R., Ex. Doc. 153, 49th Cong., 1st Sess.

In this report, it is among other things stated, that while shaping a course for St. Paul a special look-out was kept for vessels sealing.

The Captain writes:—

"While we were in the vicinity of the seal islands a look-out was kept at masthead for vessels cruizing, sealing, or illicitly trading *among those islands*. But no such vessels were seen."

Having drawn attention to the number of vessels which had taken, or had endeavoured to take seals on the shores of the islands, and illustrated the great difficulty of preventing the landing thereupon, the Commander concludes as follows:—

"In view of the foregoing facts, I would respectfully suggest—

"1. That the Department cause to be printed in the Western papers, particularly those of San Francisco, California, and Victoria, British Columbia, the sections of the law relating to the killing of fur-bearing animals in Alaskan waters, and defining in specific terms what is meant by Alaskan waters.

"2. That a revenue-cutter be sent to cruize in the vicinity of the Pribyloff Islands and Aleutian group during the sealing season."

[348] R

On the 6th March, 1886, Mr. Daniel Manning, Secretary to the Treasury, wrote to the Collector of Customs at San Francisco as follows:— *Senate, Ex. Doc., 50th Cong., 2nd Sess., No. 106, p. 135.*

"*Treasury Department,*
"Sir, "*March 6, 1886.*

"I transmit herewith, for your information, a copy of a letter addressed by the Department on the 12th March, 1881, to D. A. d'Ancona, concerning the jurisdiction of the United States in the waters of the Territory of Alaska, and the prevention of the killing of fur-seals and other fur-bearing animals within such areas, as prescribed by chapter 3, title 23, of the Revised Statutes. The attention of your predecessor in office was called to this subject on the 4th April, 1881. This communication is addressed to you, inasmuch as it is understood that certain parties at your port contemplate the fitting out of expeditions to kill fur-seals in these waters. You are requested to give due publicity to such letters, in order that such parties may be informed of the construction placed by this Department upon the provision of law referred to. *See ante, p. 111.*

"Yours, &c.
(Signed) "D. MANNING,
"*Secretary.*"

Public notice appears to have been given accordingly in the terms of the letter addressed by Mr. H. F. French to Mr. d'Ancona. (See *ante*, p. 111.) *Blue Book, "United States No. 2 (1890)," p. 7. See Appendix, vol. iii.*

The statement of facts in this chapter establishes:—

That from the year 1867 down to the year 1886 the action of the United States and Russia, the parties to the Treaty of Cession of 1867, is consistent only with the view that the rights possessed by the United States and by Russia respectively in the waters of Behring Sea were only those ordinarily incident to the possession of the coasts of that sea and the islands situated therein.

That during that period, notwithstanding the presence of seal-hunting craft in Behring Sea, the United States' authorities confined the exercise of jurisdiction to the land and waters included within the ordinary territorial limits.

CHAPTER VII.

HEAD (G).—*Various Contentions of the United States since the year 1886.*

ions of United States since 1886. The considerable development of pelagic sealing in the North Pacific which had taken place in the years previous to 1886 had established a very strong competition against the Alaska Commercial Company. That Company, paying a considerable royalty to the United States' Government upon every skin, had now to face the competition of the pelagic sealers, who paid no rent or royalty. The Company therefore exerted all its influence, especially powerful at Washington, to check and, if possible, destroy this competition. Till the development of the pelagic sealing industry, the actual circumstances had been such as to allow the Company largely to control the markets for seal-skins, and to enable them to exercise a practical monopoly of sealing in the North Pacific.

ructions to revenue-cutters. In the year 1886 the United States' Government for the first time furnished revenue-cutters with instructions to prevent any vessel from sealing in any part of Behring Sea to the eastward of the geographical limit mentioned in the Treaty of Cession.

Reports of Governor of Alaska, 1886, p. 48; 1887, p. 36. Blue Book, "United States No. 2 (1890)," p. 45. See Appendix, vol. iii.

This action by the United States was the first attempt to actively interfere with the right of the vessels of other nations to navigate and fish in the waters of Behring Sea other than territorial waters.

ure of three British vessels.

See Judge Dawson's summing up in case of "Thornton," Blue Book, "United States No. 2 (1890)," p. 30. See Appendix, vol. iii.

In pursuance of the above-mentioned orders, three British vessels were seized during this year while fishing outside ordinary territorial waters, and subsequently condemned upon the ground that the waters in which they were fishing, formed part of the waters of Alaska and were subject to the jurisdiction of the United States.

test of British Government. Sir L. S. Sackville West, British Minister at Washington, at once, by instruction, made a formal protest in the name of Her Majesty's Government against these seizures of British vessels.

[248] R 2

Attorney-General Garland issued the following order, after the British protest:— 50th Cong., 2nd Sess., Senate Ex. Doc. No. 106, p. 185.

"*Washington, D.C., January 26*, 1887.

"Judge Lafayette Dawson and M. D. Ball, United States' District Attorney, Sitka, Alaska.

" I am directed by the President to instruct you to discontinue any further proceedings in the matter of the seizure of the British vessels 'Carolena,' 'Onward,' and 'Thornton,' and discharge all vessels now held under such seizure, and release all persons that may be under arrest in connection therewith.

(Signed) " A. H. GARLAND,
"*Attorney-General.*"

Mr. Bayard, however, the Secretary of State, wrote, on the 3rd February, 1887, to Sir L. S. Sackville West that this order was issued "without conclusion of any questions which may be found to be involved in these cases of seizure." Ibid., p. 40.

Fresh seizures took place in July and August of 1887, and renewed protest was made by Great Britain. Renewed seizures.

No seizure occurred in 1888, though British sealing-vessels made large catches in that year in Behring Sea.

In 1889 five British ships were seized in Behring Sea, and three others were ordered out of the sea.

In 1890 no seizures were made, though a largre number of sealers visited the sea and took seals therein.

In 1891 an agreement was come to between the United States and Great Britain, resulting in a *modus vivendi*, for the purpose of temporarily regulating the fishery, pending the result of expert investigation into the necessities of the case. Vessels were forbidden to take seals in Behring Sea for a limited period under penalty of seizure and fine, and, on the other hand, the number allowed to be killed on the islands was largely reduced. The only seizures that have occurred since the establishment of the *modus vivendi* have been made on the ground of its infraction.[*] "Modus Vivendi." Blue Book, "United States No. 3 (1892)," p. 39. See Appendix, vol. iii.

---

[*] See Table on opposite page.

The legality of the seizures made in 1886, 1887, and 1889 became a subject of much discussion and debate in the United States. The uncertainty of the claim of the Government of the United States is exemplified by the fact that United States' sealers entered Behring Sea to seal three or four years before the British sealers entered, and they rapidly increased in numbers, but were only occasionally interfered with or seized.

in Congress of rights of United States.

H. R., 50th Cong., 2nd Sess., Report No. 3883, p. 1. To accompany Bill H. R. 12432.

During the fiftieth Session of the House of Representatives, in 1889, the Committee on Marine and Fisheries was directed "to fully investigate and report upon the nature and extent of the rights and interests of the United States in the fur-seals and other fisheries in the Behring Sea in Alaska, whether and to what extent the same had been violated, and by whom; and what, if

---

* The following Table shows the names of the British sealing-vessels seized or warned by United States' revenue cruisers 1886-90, and the approximate distance from land when seized. The distances assigned in the cases of the "Carolena," "Thornton," and "Onward" are on the authority of U. S. Naval Commander Abbey (see 50th Cong., 2nd Sess., Senate Ex. Doc. No. 106, pp. 20, 40, 30). The distances assigned in the cases of the "Anna Beck," "W. P. Sayward," "Dolphin," and "Grace" are on the authority of Captain Shepard, U. S. R. M. (Blue Book, "United States No. 2 (1890)," pp. 80-82. See Appendix, vol. iii).

Name of Vessel.	Date of Seizure.	Approximate Distance from Land when seized.	United States' Vessel making Seizure.
Carolena	August 1, 1886	75 miles	Corwin.
Thornton	" 1, "	70 "	"
Onward	" 2, "	115 "	"
Favourite	" 2, "	Warned by "Corwin" in about same position as "Onward."	
Anna Beck	July 2, 1887	66 miles	Rush.
W. P. Sayward	" 9, "	59 "	"
Dolphin	" 12, "	40 "	"
Grace	" 17, "	96 "	"
Alfred Adams	August 10, "	62 "	"
Ada	" 25, "	15 "	Bear.
Triumph	" 4, "	Warned by "Rush" not to enter Behring Sea.	
Juanita	July 31, 1889	66 miles	Rush.
Pathfinder	" 29, "	50 "	"
Triumph	" 11, "	Ordered out of Behring Sea by "Rush." [?] As to position when warned.	
Black Diamond	" 11, "	35 miles	"
Lily	August 6, "	66 "	"
Ariel	July 30, "	Ordered out of Behring Sea by "Rush."	
Kate	August 13, "	Ditto ..	"
Minnie	July 15, "	65 miles	"
Pathfinder	March 27, 1890	Seized in Neah Bay†	Corwin.

† Neah Bay is in the State of Washington, and the "Pathfinder" was seized there on charges made against her in Behring Sea in the previous year. She was released two days later.

any, legislation is necessary for the better protection and preservation of the same."

The Committee reported, upholding the claim of the United States to jurisdiction over all waters and land included in the geographical limits stated in the Treaty of Cession by Russia to the United States, and construing different Acts of Congress as perfecting the claim of national territorial rights over the open waters of Behring Sea everywhere within the above-mentioned limits.

Report of Committee of House of Representatives.

The Report states:—

"The territory of Alaska consists of land and water. Exclusive of its lakes, rivers, harbours, and inlets, there is a large area of marine territory which lies outside of the 3-mile limit from the shore, but is within the boundary-lines of the territory transferred by Russia to the United States."

H. R., 50th Cong., 2nd Sess., Report No. 3883, p. 10.

* * * *

The concluding portion of the Report states as follows:—

"That the chief object of the purchase of Alaska was the acquisition of the valuable products of Behring Sea.

Ibid., p. 23.

"That at the date of the cession of Alaska to the United States, Russia's title to Behring Sea was perfect and undisputed.

"That by virtue of the Treaty of Cession, the United States acquired complete title to all that portion of Behring Sea situated within the limits prescribed by the Treaty.

"The Committee herewith report a bill making necessary amendments of the existing law relating to these subjects, and recommend its passage."

The Report describes these amendments as declaring—

"The true meaning and intent of section 1956 of the Revised Statutes which prohibit the killing of fur-seals, &c., in the waters of Alaska, and requires the President to issue an annual Proclamation, and cause one or more Government vessels to cruize said waters, in order to prohibit the unlawful killing of fur-seals therein.

Ibid., p. 24.

"The amendment increases the revenues of the Government from this source by at least 150,000 dollars per annum."

The Bill reported contained the following Section:—

"Section 2. That section 1956 of the Revised Statutes of the United States was intended to include and apply, and is hereby declared to include and apply, to *all the waters of Behring Sea in Alaska embraced within the boundary-lines mentioned and described in the Treaty with Russia*, dated the 30th March, A.D. 1867, by which the Territory of Alaska was ceded to the United States;

Bill H. R., 12432. Blue Book, "United States No. 2 (1890)," p. 248 See Appendix, vol. iii.

and it shall be the duty of the President, at a timely season in each year, to issue his Proclamation, and cause the same to be published for one month in at least one newspaper published at each United States' port of entry on the Pacific coast, warning all persons against entering said Territory and waters for the purpose of violating the provisions of said Section; and he shall also cause one or more vessels of the United States to diligently cruize said waters and arrest all persons, and seize all vessels found to be, or to have been, engaged in any violation of the laws of the United States therein."

Conference of the Houses.

Mr. Edwardes to Lord Salisbury, March 23, 1889. Blue Book, "United States No. 2 (1890)," p. 243. See Appendix, vol. iii.

This Bill did not pass the House of Representatives, but the above section was added by the House as an amendment to a Bill for the "Protection of the Salmon Fisheries of Alaska," which originated in the Senate. The Senate, however, refused to accept the House amendment, and the Bill was accordingly referred to a conference of the Houses, and the section, as finally modified and adopted in the Act of the 2nd March, 1889, reads as follows:—

Ibid., p. 237.

"Section 3. That section 1956 of the Revised Statutes of the United States is hereby declared to include and apply to *all the dominion of the United States in the waters of Behring Sea*, and it shall be the duty of the President, at a timely season in each year, to issue his Proclamation, and cause the same to be published for one month in at least one newspaper (if any such there be) published in each United States' port of entry on the Pacific coast, warning all persons against entering said waters for the purpose of violating the provisions of said section, and he shall cause one or more vessels of the United States to diligently cruize said waters, and arrest all persons and seize all vessels found to be or to have been engaged in any violation of the laws of the United States therein."

Ibid., p. 234.

On the 21st March, 1889, President Harrison issued his Proclamation accordingly, warning "all persons against entering the waters of Behring Sea within the domain of the United States for the purpose of violating the provisions of said Section 1956 of Revised Statutes."

International Agreement proposed.

International Agreement proposed.

On the 19th August, 1887, after the seizure of the "W. P. Sayward," and while she was in custody, the United States' Secretary of State wrote identic instructions to the United States' Ministers in France, Germany, Great Britain,[*]

[*] The invitation conveyed by the instructions was not, however, communicated to Great Britain until November 11, 1887. See 50th Cong., 2nd Sess., Senate Ex. Doc. No. 106, p. 87; and Blue Book, "United States No. 2 (1890);" Sir J. Pauncefote to Baron Plessen, October 11, 1887. See Appendix, vol. iii.

Japan, Russia, and Sweden and Norway in the following terms:—

International Agreement proposed

"Recent occurrences have drawn the attention of this Department to the necessity of taking steps for the better protection of the fur-seal fisheries in Bering Sea. Without raising any question as to the exceptional measures which the particular character of the property in question might justify this Government in taking, and without reference to any exceptional marine jurisdiction that might properly be claimed for that end, it is deemed advisable—and I am instructed by the President so to inform you—to attain the desired ends by international co-operation.

Senate, Ex. Doc., 50th Cong., 2nd Sess., No. 106, p. 84.

"It is well known that the unregulated and indiscriminate killing of seals in many parts of the world has driven them from place to place, and, by breaking up their habitual resorts, has greatly reduced their number.

"Under these circumstances, and in view of the *common interests* of *all nations* in preventing the indiscriminate destruction and consequent extermination of an animal which contributes so importantly to the *commercial wealth* and *general use of mankind*, you are hereby instructed to draw the attention of the Government to which you are accredited to the subject, and *invite* it to enter *into such an arrangement* with the Government of the United States as will prevent the citizens of either country from killing seal in Bering Sea at such times and places, and by such methods as at present are pursued, and which threaten the speedy extermination of those animals and consequent serious *loss to mankind*.

"The Ministers of the United States to Germany, Sweden and Norway, Russia, Japan, and Great Britain have been each similarly addressed on the subject referred to in this instruction."

So to Mr. White, Secretary of the United States' Legation in London, with reference to this proposition, he wrote, on the 1st May, 1888:—

"The suggestion made by Lord Salisbury, that it may be necessary to bring other Governments than the United States, Great Britain, and Russia into the arrangements, has already been met by the action of the Department, as I have heretofore informed you. At the same time, the invitation was sent to the British Government to negotiate a Convention for seal protection in Bering Sea, a like invitation was extended to various other Powers, which have, without exception, returned a favourable response.

Ibid., p. 101.

"In order, therefore, that the plan may be carried out, the Convention proposed between the United States, Great Britain, and Russia should contain a clause providing for the subsequent adhesion of other Powers."

And on the 7th February, 1888, the Secretary of State, in a despatch to the Minister at the

Court of St. James', after referring to the killing of seals in Behring Sea, wrote:—

50th Cong., 2nd Sess., Senate Ex. Doc. No. 106, p. 89.

"The only way of obviating the lamentable result above predicted appears to be by the United States, Great Britain, and other interested Powers taking concerted action to prevent their citizens or subjects from killing fur seals with fire-arms or other destructive weapons, north of 50° of north latitude, and between 160° of longitude west and 170° of longitude east from Greenwich, during the period intervening between April 15 and November 1."

Contentions of the United States.

Contentions of the United States.

Judge Dawson's directions to the jury. Case of the "Thornton."

Blue Book, "United States No. 2 (1890)," p. 21. See Appendix, vol. III.

The Judge of the District Court of Alaska, the Honourable Lafayette Dawson, is reported, in summing up the case to the jury, to have quoted the 1st Article of the Treaty of Cession of the 30th March, 1867, and to have continued as follows:—

"All the waters within the boundary set forth in this Treaty to the western end of the Aleutian Archipelago and chain of islands are to be considered as comprised within the waters of Alaska, and all the penalties prescribed by law against the killing of fur-bearing animals must therefore attach against any violation of law within the limits heretofore described.

Claim of jurisdiction in Behring Sea east of 193° west longitude.

"If, therefore, the jury believe from the evidence that the defendants did by themselves or in conjunction with others, on or about the time charged in the information, kill any otter, mink, marten, sable, or fur-seal, or other fur-bearing animal or animals, on the shores of Alaska, or in the Behring Sea, east of the 193° of west longitude, the jury should find the defendants guilty, and assess their punishment separately, at a fine of not less than 200 dollars nor more than 1,000 dollars, or imprisonment not more than six months, or by both, such fines within the limits herein set forth, and imprisonment."

Case of the "Anna Beck" and other vessels. Brief for United States' Government.

The Counsel appearing for the United States' Government, to justify the seizure of the "Anna Beck" and other vessels in 1887, filed a "brief," from which the following extracts are taken:—

See Blue Book, "United States No. 2 (1890)," p. 112. See Appendix, vol. III.

"The information in this case is based on section 1956 of chapter 3 of the Revised Statutes of the United States, which provides that—

"'No person shall kill any otter, mink, marten, sable, or fur-seal, or other fur-bearing animal within the limits of Alaska Territory or in the waters thereof.'

"The offence is charged to have been committed 130 miles north of the Island of Ounalaska, and therefore in the main waters of that part of the Behring Sea ceded by Russia to the United States by the Treaty of 1867.

The defendants demur to the information on the ground—

"1. That the Court has no jurisdiction over the defendants, the alleged offence having been committed beyond the limit of a marine league from the shores of Alaska.

"2. That the Act under which the defendants were arrested is unconstitutional in so far as it restricts the free navigation of the Behring Sea for fishing and sealing purposes beyond the limits of a marine league from shore. The issue thus raised by the demurrer presents squarely the questions:—

"(1.) The jurisdiction of the United States over Behring Sea.

"(2.) The power of Congress to legislate concerning those waters.

"*The Argument.*

"The fate of the second of these propositions depends largely upon that of the first, for if the jurisdiction and dominion of the United States as to these waters be not sustained the restrictive Acts of Congress must fall, and if our jurisdiction shall be sustained small question can be made as to the power of Congress to regulate fishing and sealing within our own waters. The grave question, one important to all the nations of the civilized world, as well as to the United States and Great Britain, is 'the dominion of Behring Sea.'"

After conceding unreservedly the general doctrine of the 3-mile limit, he proceeds:—

"It thus appears that from our earliest history, contemporaneously with our acceptance of the principle of the marine league belt and supported by the same high authorities is the assertion of the doctrine of our right to dominion over our inland waters under the Treaty of 1867, and on this rule of international law we base our claim to jurisdiction and dominion over the waters of the Behring Sea. While it is, no doubt, true that a nation cannot by Treaty acquire dominion in contravention of the law of nations, it is none the less true that, whatever title or dominion our grantor, Russia, possessed under the law of nations at the time of the Treaty of Cession in 1867, passed and now rightfully belongs to the United States. Having determined the law, we are next led to inquire as to whether Behring Sea is an inland water or a part of the open ocean, and what was Russia's jurisdiction over it.

"Behring Sea is an inland water. Beginning on the eastern coast of Asia, this body of water, formerly known as the Sea of Kamtchatka, is bounded by the Peninsula of Kamtchatka and Eastern Siberia to the Behring Strait. From the American side of this strait the waters of the Behring Sea wash the coast of the mainland of Alaska as far south as the Peninsula of Alaska. From the extremity of this peninsula, in a long, sweeping curve, the Aleutian

Case of the "Anna Beck" and other vessels. Brief for United States Government.

Behring Sea said to be inland wa

Islands stretch in a continuous chain almost to the shores of Kamtchatka, thus encasing the sea."

And he concludes:—

"Enough has been said to disclose the basis of Russia's right to jurisdiction of the Behring Sea under the law of nations, viz., original possession of the Asiatic coast, followed by discovery and possession of the Aleutian chain and the shores of Alaska north, not only to Behring Strait, but to Point Barrow and the Frozen Ocean, thus inclosing within its territory, as within the embrace of a mighty giant, the islands and waters of Behring Sea, and with this the assertion and exercise of dominion over land and sea.

"Such is our understanding of the law, such is the record. Upon them the United States are prepared to abide the Judgments of the Courts and the opinion of the civilized world."

Blue Book, "United States No. 2 (1890)," p. 89. See Appendix, vol. iii.

On the 10th September, 1887, the Marquis of Salisbury, addressing Sir Lionel West, British Minister at Washington, discussed the proceedings in the United States' District Court in the cases of the "Carolena," "Onward," and "Thornton." After stating that Her Majesty's Government could not find in these proceedings any justification for the condemnation of those vessels, he wrote:—

Blue Book, "United States No. 2 (1890)," p. 89. See Appendix, vol. iii.

"The libels of information allege that they were seized for killing fur-seal within the limits of Alaska Territory, and in the waters thereof, in violation of section 1956 of the Revised Statutes of the United States; and the United States' Naval Commander Abbey certainly affirmed that the vessels were seized within the waters of Alaska and the Territory of Alaska; but according to his own evidence, they were seized 75, 115, and 70 miles respectively south-south-east of St. George's Island.

"It is not disputed, therefore, that the seizures in question were effected at a distance from land far in excess of the limit of maritime jurisdiction which any nation can claim by international law, and it is hardly necessary to add that such limit cannot be enlarged by any municipal law.

"The claim thus set up appears to be founded on the exceptional title said to have been conveyed to the United States by Russia at the time of the cession of the Alaska Territory. The pretension which the Russian Government at one time put forward to exclusive jurisdiction over the whole of Behring Sea was, however, never admitted either by this country or by the United States of America."

Upon this ground the discussion between Her Majesty's Government and the Government of the United States was carried on for some years until the receipt of Mr. Blaine's despatch of the 22nd January, 1890, to Sir Julian Pauncefote, the British Minister at Washington, wherein a new or modified position was taken up, and it was asserted to be *contra bonos mores* to engage in the killing of seals at sea.

Mr. Blaine, after promising Sir Julian Pauncefote to put in writing the precise grounds upon which the United States justified the seizures, wrote as follows:—

    Mr. Blaine upon the seizures.

"In the opinion of the President, the Canadian vessels arrested and detained in the Behring Sea were engaged in a pursuit that is in itself *contra bonos mores*—a pursuit which of necessity involves a serious and permanent injury to the rights of the Government and people of the United States.

    Sealing *contra bonos mores*.

    Mr. Blaine to Sir J. Pauncefote, January 22, 1890. Blue Book, "United States No. 2 (1890)," p. 396. See Appendix, vol. iii.

"To establish this ground, it is not necessary to argue the question of the extent and nature of the sovereignty of this Government over the waters of the Behring Sea; it is not necessary to explain, certainly not to define, the powers and privileges ceded by His Imperial Majesty the Emperor of Russia in the Treaty, by which the Alaskan Territory was transferred to the United States. The weighty consideration growing out of the acquisition of that territory, with all the rights on land and sea inseparably connected therewith, may be safely left out of view while the grounds are set forth upon which this Government rests its justification for the action complained of by Her Majesty's Government."....

He argues that the practice of pelagic sealing insures the extermination of the species, and continues:—

"In the judgment of this Government, the law of the sea is not lawlessness. Nor can the law of the sea and the liberty which it confers and which it protects be perverted to justify acts which are immoral in themselves, which inevitably tend to result against the interest and against the welfare of mankind. One step beyond that which Her Majesty's Government has taken in this contention, and piracy finds its justification."

    Ibid., p. 398.

On the 17th December, 1890, Mr. Blaine again wrote to Sir Julian Pauncefote:—

    Behring Sea not included in Pacific Ocean in Treaties of 1824 and 1825.

"Legal and diplomatic questions, apparently complicated, are often found, after prolonged discussion, to depend on the settlement of a single point. Such, in the judgment of the President, is the position in which the United States and Great Britain find themselves in the pending controversy touching the true construction of the Russo-American and Anglo-Russian Treaties of 1824 and 1825. Great Britain contends that the phrase 'Pacific Ocean,' as used in the Treaties, was intended to include,

    Blue Book, "United States No. 1 (1891)," pp. 37, 38. See Appendix, vol.iii.

and does include, the body of water which is now known as the Behring Sea. The United States contends that the Behring Sea was not mentioned, or even referred to, in either Treaty, and was in no sense included in the phrase 'Pacific Ocean.' If Great Britain can maintain her position that the Behring Sea at the time of the Treaties with Russia of 1824 and 1825 was included in the Pacific Ocean, the Government of the United States has no well-grounded complaint against her. If, on the other hand, this Government can prove beyond all doubt that the Behring Sea, at the date of the Treaties, was understood by the three Signatory Powers to be a separate body of water, and was not included in the phrase 'Pacific Ocean,' then the American Case against Great Britain is complete and undeniable." ....

Disavowal of *mare clausum*.

Blue Book, "United States No. 1 (1891)," p. 56. See Appendix, vol. iii.

In the same note Mr. Blaine disavows the contention that the Behring Sea is *mare clausum*, but claims that the Ukase, which asserted exclusive jurisdiction over 100 miles from the coast in that Sea, was never annulled by Russia. He had in this note previously argued "that Great Britain and the United States recognized, respected, and obeyed the authority of Russia in the Behring Sea" for more than forty years after the Treaties with Russia. In conclusion, he claims for the United States the right to hold for a specific purpose a "comparatively restricted area of water."

Ibid., p. 41.

Ukase of 1821 never annulled in Behring Sea.

In this note the Secretary of State thus expresses himself:—

Ibid., p. 52.

"The English statesmen of that day had, as I have before remarked, attempted the abolition of the Ukase of Alexander only so far as it affected the coast of the Pacific Ocean from the 51st to the 60th degree of north latitude. It was left in full force on the shores of the Behring Sea. There is no proof whatever that the Russian Emperor annulled it there. That sea, from east to west, is 1,300 miles in extent; from north to south it is 1,000 miles in extent. The whole of this great body of water, under the Ukase, was left open to the world, except a strip of 100 miles from the shore. But with these 100 miles enforced on all the coasts of the Behring Sea, it would be obviously impossible to approach the Straits of Behring, which were less than 50 miles in extreme width." ....

to control restricted area for specific purpose.

Ibid., p. 54.

"The United States desires only such control over a limited extent of the waters in the Behring Sea, for a part of each year, as will be sufficient to insure the protection of the fur-seal fisheries, already injured, possibly, to an irreparable extent, by the intrusion of Canadian vessels'

* * * *

Ibid., p. 56.

"The repeated assertions that the Government of the United States demands that the Behring Sea be pronounced *mare clausum* are without foundation. The Government has never claimed it, and never desired it. It expressly disavows it.

"At the same time the United States does not lack abundant authority, according to the ablest exponents of international law, for holding a small section of the Behring Sea for the protection of the fur-seals. Controlling a comparatively restricted area of water for that one specific purpose is by no means the equivalent of declaring the sea, or any part thereof, *mare clausum.*"

This disavowal of any claim to Behring Sea as a *mare clausum* is again referred to in Mr. Blaine's despatch of the 14th April, 1891.

On the 21st February, 1891, in answer to the despatch of Mr. Blaine of the 17th December, 1890, Lord Salisbury wrote to Sir Julian Pauncefote:—

Blue Book, "United States No. 3 (1892)," p. 2. See Appendix, vol. iii.

"The effect of . . . ssion which has been carried on between the two G.. .nments has been materially to narrow the area of controversy. It is now quite clear that the advisers of the President do not claim Behring Sea as a *mare clausum,* and indeed that they repudiate that contention in express terms. Nor do they rely, as a justification for the seizure of British ships in the open sea, upon the contention that the interests of the seal fisheries give to the United States' Government any right for that purpose which, according to international law, it would not otherwise possess. Whatever importance they attach to the preservation of the fur-seal species,—and they justly look on it as an object deserving the most serious solicitude,— they do not conceive that it confers upon any Maritime Power rights over the open ocean which that Power could not assert on other grounds.

Blue Book, "United States No. 1 (1891)," p. 87. See Appendix, vol. iii.

"The claim of the United States to prevent the exercise of the seal fishery by other nations in Behring Sea rests now exclusively upon the interest which by purchase they possess in a Ukase issued by the Emperor Alexander I in the year 1821, which prohibits foreign vessels from approaching within 100 Italian miles of the coasts and islands then belonging to Russia in Behring Sea."

In reply to this, Mr. Blaine wrote on the 14th April, 1891:—

"In the opinion of the President, Lord Salisbury is wholly and strangely in error in making the following statement: 'Nor do they [the advisers of the President] rely as a justification for the seizure of British ships in the open sea upon the contention that the interests of the seal fisheries give to the United States' Government any right for that purpose which, according to international law, it would not otherwise possess.' The Government of the United States has steadily held just the reverse of the position Lord Salisbury has imputed to it. It holds that the ownership of the islands upon which the seals breed, that the habit of the seals in regularly resorting thither

Blue Book, "United States No. 3 (1892)," p. 4. See Appendix, vol. iii.

of property interest in seals.

and rearing their young thereon, that their going out from the islands in search of food and regularly returning thereto, and all the facts and incidents of their relation to the islands, give to the United States a property interest therein; that this property interest was claimed and exercised by Russia during the whole period of its sovereignty over the land and waters of Alaska; that England recognized this property interest, so far as recognition is implied by abstaining from all interference with it during the whole period of Russia's ownership of Alaska, and during the first nineteen years of the sovereignty of the United States.

"It is yet to be determined whether the lawless intrusion of Canadian vessels in 1886 and subsequent years has changed the law and equity of the case theretofore prevailing."

It does not appear, however, that the special rights now apparently claimed by the United States in respect of a special property in fur-seals have ever been otherwise advanced or more definitely formulated than as above mentioned.

; of the "W. P. Sayward."

Stenographic Report of Arguments in Case of the "W. P. Sayward," p. 96.

See also Brief for United States, *ex parte* T. H. Cooper, owner and claimant of the schooner "W. P. Sayward," p. 166.

In 1891, in the course of the Argument before the Supreme Court of the United States in the case of the "W. P. Sayward," one of the learned Judges inquired of Mr. Attorney-General Miller:—

"Do you mean that the Political Department has decided in terms what constitute the waters of Alaska, or only that the United States has jurisdiction over certain waters for certain purposes?"

of territorial jurisdiction over 100 miles.

To which Mr. Miller replied:—

"That is what I understand they have decided; that they have jurisdiction, and that they have territorial jurisdiction over those waters to the extent of 100 miles."

Judgment United States' Supreme Court, *ex parte* T. H. Cooper, owner and claimant of the schooner "W. P. Sayward," p. 16.

Mr. Chief Justice Fuller, delivering the opinion of the Supreme Court of the United States in the case of the "W. P. Sayward," on the 20th February, 1892, referred to the seizures in the following terms:—

"If we assume that the record shows the locality of the alleged offence and seizure as stated, it also shows that officers of the United States, acting under the orders of their Government, seized this vessel engaged in catching seal, and took her into the nearest port; and that the Law Officers of the Government libelled her and proceeded against her for the violation of the laws of the United States, in the District Court, resulting in her condemnation.

"How did it happen that the officers received such orders? It must be admitted that they were given in the assertion on the part of this Government of territorial jurisdiction over Behring Sea to an extent exceeding 50 miles from the shores of Alaska;* that this territorial jurisdiction, in the enforcement of the laws protecting seal fisheries, was asserted by actual seizures during the seasons of 1886, 1887, and 1889, of a number of British vessels; that the Government persistently maintains that such jurisdiction belongs to it, based not only on the peculiar nature of the seal fisheries and the property of the Government in them, but also upon the position that this jurisdiction was asserted by Russia for more than ninety years, and by that Government transferred to the United States; and that negotiations are pending upon the subject."

The facts stated in this chapter show :—

That the original ground upon which the vessels seized in 1886 and 1887 were condemned, was that Behring Sea was a *mare clausum*, an inland sea, and as such had been conveyed, in part, by Russia to the United States.

That this ground was subsequently entirely abandoned, but a claim was then made to exclusive jurisdiction over 100 miles from the coast-line of the United States' territory.

That subsequently a further claim has been set up to the effect that the United States have property in and a right of protection over fur-seals in non-territorial waters.

---

* The Supreme Court, however, expressed no opinion as to the egal validity of the jurisdiction so asserted.

CHAPTER VIII.

Right of protection or property in seals outside 3-mile limit.

POINT 5 OF ARTICLE VI.—*Has the United States any Right, and, if so, what Right of Protection or Property in the Fur-Seals frequenting the Islands of the United States in Behring Sea when such seals are found outside the ordinary 3-mile limit?*

A novel claim.

The claim involved in this question is not only new in the present discussion, but is entirely without precedent. It is, moreover, in contradiction of the position assumed by the United States in analogous cases on more than one occasion.

The claim appears to be, in this instance, made only in respect of seals, but the principle involved in it might be extended on similar grounds to other animals *feræ naturæ*, such, for instance, as whales, walrus, salmon, and marine animals of many kinds.

Apart from the ordinary limits of territorial jurisdiction over waters adjacent to coasts, or to some exceptional condition based upon agreement, there is absolutely no precedent for the assumption of the right to property in a free-swimming animal, whose movements are uncontrolled and not controllable by man.

Fur-seals are indisputably animals *feræ naturæ*, and such animals have been universally regarded by jurists as *res nullius* until they are captured. No person can have property in them until he has actually reduced them into possession by capture.

Why should there be a property in seals in Behring Sea alone? Outside Behring Sea citizens of the United States have pursued the seals for years as Canadians have done, and are doing, without let or hindrance, and with the full knowledge of the United States' Government.

The proposition that on one side of the Aleutian Archipelago a seal is the property of the United States, and on the other it is the property of any man who can catch it, can only be supported on the ground that Behring Sea is the domain of the United States, in other words, a *mare clausum*.

Claim involves mare clausum.

It is, moreover, submitted that if seals before capture constitute special property, the larceny of a seal on the high seas by a vessel not belonging to the United States is not cognizable by the United States' Courts, and that any claim to protection of seals beyond territorial jurisdiction must involve *mare clausum*.

Whatever arguments may be brought forward in order to induce other nations to concur in the adoption of Regulations limiting and interfering with their rights to fish for and catch seals or other animals *feræ naturæ* upon the high seas, no nation under the principles of law and the practice among nations can, without the concurrence of all interested Powers, interfere with vessels engaged in this pursuit when outside of the ordinary territorial jurisdiction.

The principle suggested in the question discussed in this chapter has been steadily resisted by all nations. The Government of the United States has more than once distinctly asserted the principle that the fur-seal fishery is part of the ocean fishery, and free to all beyond the 3-mile limit. *Freedom of seal fisheries asserted by United States.*

In 1832 the United States' schooner "Harriet," Davison, master, was seized by the Government of the Republic of Buenos Ayres at the Falkland Islands; that Government having claimed the right to capture and detain United States' vessels engaged in the seal fishery at the Malvinas (Falkland Islands) and the islands and coasts adjacent to Cape Horn. *Falkland Islands. Case of the "Harriet".*

The United States' Chargé d'Affaires wrote, on the 20th June, 1832, to the Buenos Ayres Minister as follows:—

". . . . The Undersigned is instructed and authorized to say,—that they utterly deny the existence of any right in this Republic to interrupt, molest, detain, or capture any vessels belonging to citizens of the United States of America, or any persons being citizens of those States, engaged in taking seals, or whales, or any species of fish or marine animals, in any of the waters, or on any of the shores or lands, of any or either of the Falkland Islands, Tierra del Fuego, Cape Horn, or any of the adjacent islands in the Atlantic Ocean." British and Foreign State Papers, by Hertslet, vol. xx, p. 335.

On the 10th July, 1832, the United States' Chargé d'Affaires wrote to the same Minister as follows:

"But again,—if it be admitted, hypothetically, that the Argentine Republic did succeed to the entire rights of Spain over these regions; and that when she succeeded, Spain was possessed of sovereign rights;—the question is certainly worth examination, whether the right to exclude American vessels and American citizens from the fisheries there is incident to such a succession to sovereignty. Ibid., p. 349.

Falkland Islands seal fisheries.

"The ocean fishery is a natural right, which all nations may enjoy in common. Every interference with it by a foreign Power, is a national wrong. When it is carried on within the marine league of the coast, which has been designated as the extent of national jurisdiction, reason seems to dictate a restriction, if, under pretext of carrying on the fishery, an evasion of the Revenue Laws of the country may reasonably be apprehended, or any other serious injury to the Sovereign of the coast, he has a right to prohibit it; but, as such prohibition derogates from a natural right, the evil to be apprehended ought to be a real, not an imaginary one. No such evil can be apprehended on a desert and uninhabited coast; therefore, such coasts form no exception to the common right of Fishing in the seas adjoining them. All the reasoning on this subject applies to the large bays of the Ocean, the entrance to which cannot be defended; and this is the doctrine of Vattel, chapter 23, section 291, who expressly cites the Straits of Magellan, as an instance for the application of the rule.

British and Foreign State Papers, by Hertslet, vol. xx, p. 351.

".... The Treaty concluded between Great Britain and Spain, in 1790, already alluded to, is to be viewed, in reference to this subject, because, both nations, by restricting themselves from forming Settlements, evidently intended that the fishery should be left open, both in the waters and on the shores of these islands, and perfectly free, so that no individual claim for damage, for use of the shores, should ever arise. That case, however, could scarcely occur, for whales are invariably taken at sea, and generally without the marine league—and seals, on rocks and sandy beaches, incapable of cultivation. The Stipulation in the Treaty of 1790 is, clearly, founded on the right to use the unsettled shores for the purpose of fishery, and to secure its continuance."

Mr. Robert Greenhow, whose works have already been quoted, in a series of articles on the Falkland Islands, written for "Hunt's Merchants' Magazine," in February 1842, refers to the claim set up by Buenos Ayres respecting the jurisdiction of the Republic and the application of its laws and regulations "especially those respecting the seal fishery on the coast."

Mr. Greenhow says:—

Hunt's "Merchants' Magazine," February 1842, p 137.

"To proceed another step in admissions. Supposing the Argentine Republic to have really and unquestionably inherited from Spain the sovereignty of the territories adjoining it on the south, and the contiguous islands, that Government would still want the right to extend its 'Regulations respecting the seal fishery' to the unsettled portions of the coasts of those territories. That right was indeed assumed by Spain, with many equally unjust, which were enforced so long as other nations did not find it prudent to contest them. But as the Spanish power waned, other nations claimed their imprescriptible rights;

[248]

Falkland Islands seal fisheries.

they insisted on navigating every part of the open sea, and of its unoccupied straits and harbours, with such limitations only as each might choose to admit by Treaty with another; and they resorted to the North Pacific coasts of America for trade and settlement, and to the southernmost shores of the continent for the seal fishery, without regard for the exclusive pretensions of Spain to the sovereignty of those regions. *Of the hundreds of vessels, nearly all American, which annually frequented the coasts and seas above mentioned after* 1789, *not one was captured or detained by the Spanish authorities;* and long before the revolutions in Southern America began, the prohibitory Decrees of the Court of Madrid and of its Governors, relative to those parts of the world, had become obsolete, and the warnings of its officers were treated as jests.

"The common right of all nations to navigate and fish in the open sea, and in its indefensible straits, and to use their unsettled shores for temporary purposes, is now admitted among the principal Maritime Powers; and the stipulations in Treaties on those subjects, are intended to —prevent disputes as to *what coasts are to be considered as unsettled,—what straits are indefensible,—within what distance from a settled coast the sea ceases to be open, &c.*

"The Governments of Spanish American Republics have, however, in many instances exhibited a strong indisposition to conform with these and other such Regulations of national law, though clearly founded on justice and reason, and intended clearly for the benefit of the weak, to which class they all belong."

He also refers to the case of the "Harriet" as follows:—

" .... The President at the same time declared, that the name of the Republic of Buenos Ayres 'had been used, to cover with a show of authority, acts injurious to the commerce of the United States, and to the property and liberty of their citizens; for which reason, he had given orders for the dispatch of an armed vessel to join the American squadron in the south seas, and aid in affording all lawful protection to the trade of the Union, which might be required; and he should without delay send a Minister to Buenos Ayres, to examine into the nature of the circumstances, and also of the claim set up by that Government to the Falkland Islands.

Hunt's "Merchants' Magazine," February 1842, p. 143.

" .... The question had, however, become more complicated before the arrival of Mr. Baylies at Buenos Ayres.

Ibid., p 144.

"The 'Lexington' reached Berkeley Sound on the 28th December, and lay at the entrance, during a severe gale, until the 31st, when she went up and anchored in front of the harbour of Soledad. Boats were immediately sent ashore, with armed seamen and marines, who made prisoners of Brisbane, Metcalf, and some other persons, and sent them on board the ship; the cannon mounted before the place were at the same time spiked, some of the arms and ammunition were destroyed, and the seal-skins and other articles taken from the 'Harriet' and 'Superior' were removed from the warehouses, and placed in the schooner 'Dash,' which carried them to the United States. Captain Duncan then gave notice to the inhabitants that the seal fishery on those coasts was in future to be free to all Americans; and that the capture of any vessel of the United States would be regarded as an act of piracy; and having affixed a declaration in writing to that effect on the door of the Government-house, he took his departure, on the 22nd January, 1832, carrying with him in the 'Loxington,' Brisbane and six other persons as prisoners, with many of the negroes and settlers as passengers."

Halifax Fisheries Commission
Mr. Dana's speech.

Record of the Proceedings of Halifax Fisheries Commission, 1877, p. 1653.

Mr. R. H. Dana, in his speech on behalf of the United States before the Halifax Fisheries Commission in 1887, says:—

"The right to fish in the sea is in its nature not real, as the common law has it, nor immovable, as named by the civil law, but personal. It is a liberty. It is a franchise or a faculty. It is not property pertaining to or connected with the land. It is incorporeal; it is aboriginal. The right of fishing, dropping line or net into the sea, to draw from it the means of sustenance, is as old as the human race, and the limits that have been set about it have been set about it in recent and modern times, and wherever the fisherman is excluded, a reason for excluding him should always be given. I speak of the deep sea fishermen following the free-swimming fish through the sea, not of the crustaceous animals, or of any of those that connect themselves with the soil under the sea or adjacent to the sea, nor do I speak of any fishing which requires possession of the land or any touching or troubling the bottom of the sea; I speak of the deep-sea fishermen who sail over the high seas pursuing the free-swimming fish of the high seas. Against them, it is a question not of admission, but of exclusion. These fish are not property. Nobody owns them. They come we know not whence, and go we know not whither.

*   *   *   *

"They are no man's property; they belong by right of nature to those who take them, and every man may take them who can."

Dr. Woolsey's opinion

Sec. 89, p. 73, sixth edition.

Dr. Woolsey, in the sixth edition of his Treatise on International Law, says:—

"The recent controversy between Great Britain and the United States involving the right of British subjects to catch seals in North Pacific waters appears to be an attempted revival of these old claims to jurisdiction over broad stretches of sea. That an international agreement establishing a rational close season for the fur-seal is wise and necessary no one can dispute, but to prevent foreigners from sealing on the high sea or within the Kamschatkan Sea (which is not even inclosed by American territory, its west and north-west shores being Russian) is as unwarranted as if England should warn fishermen of other nationalities off the Newfoundland banks.

In the absence of any indication as to the grounds upon which the United States base so unprecedented a claim as that of a right to protection of or property in animals *feræ naturæ* upon the high seas, the further consideration of this claim must of necessity be postponed; but it is maintained that, according to the principles of international law, no property can exist in animals *feræ naturæ* when frequenting the high seas.

CHAPTER IX.

General Conclusions upon the whole Case.

<small>General conclusions.</small>

It now remains to state the principles of law applicable to the whole Case, some authorities bearing thereon, and the conclusions of fact established by the foregoing statement, and to formulate the final propositions both of law and of fact, upon which Great Britain will insist.

<small>Behring Sea an open sea.</small>

The sea now known as Behring Sea is an open sea forming part of the common highway of all nations, and especially of Great Britain to her possessions in the northern parts of North America. In the absence of Treaty or international arrangement, all the nations of the world have the right to navigate and fish in such waters, and no mere declarations or claims by any one or more nations can take away or restrict the rights of other nations. Moreover, mere non-use or absence of the exercise by any nation of her rights cannot in any way impair or take away the right of that nation or of any other nation to exercise those rights. They are, in fact, the common heritage of all mankind, and incapable of being appropriated by any one or more nations.

<small>Kent's "Commentaries," vol. i, 9th edition, Boston, 1858, p. 29.</small>

The rights and interests of nations in the open sea are correctly stated by Chancellor Kent as follows:—

"The open sea is not capable of being possessed as private property. The free use of the ocean for navigation and fishing is common to all mankind, and the public jurists generally and explicitly deny that the main ocean can ever be appropriated."

<small>Wheaton, Elements, 8th edition by Dana, 1866, p. 269.</small>

The controversy between Grotius and Selden as to the right of appropriation by a nation of the sea beyond the immediate vicinity of the coast is thus reviewed by Wheaton:—

"There are only two decisive reasons applicable to the question. The first is physical and material, which would alone be sufficient; but when coupled with the second reason, which is purely moral, will be found conclusive of the whole controversy.

"1. Those things which are originally the common property of all mankind can only become the exclusive property of a particular individual or society of men, by means of possession. In order to establish the claim of a particular nation to a right of property in the sea, that nation must obtain and keep possession of it, which is impossible.

"2. In the second place, the sea is an element which belongs equally to all men, like the air. No nation, then, has the right to appropriate it, even though it might be physically possible to do so.

"It is thus demonstrated that the sea cannot become the exclusive property of any nation. And, consequently, the use of the sea for these purposes, remains open and common to all mankind."

Cf. Ortolan, "Diplomatie de la Mer," tom. I, pp. 120-126.

In a note on this passage of Wheaton, Mr. Dana adds that—

"The right of one nation, or of several nations, to an exclusive jurisdiction over an open sea, was, as stated in the text, rested solely on a kind of prescription. But however long acquiesced in, such an appropriation is inadmissible, in the nature of things; and whatever may be the evidence of the time or nature of the use, it is set aside as a bad usage, which no evidence can make legal."

No prescription in open sea.

Sir R. Phillimore writes:—

"The right of navigation, fishing, and the like, upon the open sea, being *jura merœ facultatis*, rights which do not require a continuous exercise to maintain their validity, but which may or may not be exercised according to the free will and pleasure of those entitled to them, can neither be lost by *non-user* or *prescribed* against, nor acquired to the exclusion of others by having been immemorially exercised by one nation only. No presumption can arise that those who have not hitherto exercised such rights, have abandoned the intention of ever doing so."

Phillimore, "International Law," 2nd edition, 1871, I, § 174.

The following position was correctly taken by the United States in 1862, and, it is presumed, will be adhered to by that country to-day.

Position taken by United States in 1862: Cuba.

In that year Spain pushed her claim to an extended jurisdiction round the Island of Cuba. Secretary Seward wrote:—

"It cannot be admitted, nor indeed is Mr. Tessara understood to claim, that the mere assertion of a Sovereign, by an act of legislation, however solemn, can have the effect to establish and fix its external maritime jurisdiction. . . . He cannot, by a mere Decree, extend the limit and fix it at 6 miles, because, if he could, he could in the same manner, and upon motives of interest, ambition, and even upon caprice, fix it at 10, or 20, or 50 miles, without the consent or acquiescence of other Powers which have a common right with himself in the freedom of all the oceans. Such a pretension could never be successfully or rightfully maintained."

Mr. Seward to Mr. Tessara. Wharton Digest of "International Law," vol. I, sec. 32, p. 103. See Blue Book, "United States No. 2 (1893)," p. 318. See Appendix, vol III.

It is claimed by Great Britain that the facts already stated establish :—

(A.) That from the earliest times down to the year 1821 the ships of Great Britain and the

Chapter I.

General conclusions.	United States and of other foreign nations navigated the non-territorial waters of Behring Sea and the other parts of the North Pacific, and exercised freely the natural and common rights therein without interference or remonstrance by Russia.
Chapter II.	(B.) That when, in the year 1821, Russia, in the terms of the Ukase of that date, advanced claims to exercise control over a considerable portion of the non-territorial waters of the North Pacific (including a large part of the non-territorial waters of Behring Sea) as over a *mare clausum*, the practice of nations and their admitted rights upon the high seas were already entirely opposed to any claim to such exclusive and exceptional rights as were embodied in or implied by the Ukase.
	That this attempt on the part of Russia led to immediate and emphatic protests by Great Britain and the United States, which protests led to the withdrawal of Russia's claims. That those claims were never recognized or conceded by Great Britain in the smallest degree.
	That, in view of the continued practice of nations and the growth of the principles of international law since 1821, the arguments then employed by Great Britain and the United States have to-day, if possible, even greater weight than at that period.
Chapter III.	(C.) That the body of water now commonly known as " Behring Sea " is included in the phrase " Pacific Ocean " as used in the Treaty of 1825 between Great Britain and Russia, and that that Treaty was intended to declare the rights of Great Britain to navigate and fish in all the waters over which Russia had attempted to control and limit such rights, that is to say, from Behring Strait on the north to latitude 51° on the coast of America, and latitude 45° 50′ on the coast of Asia.
Chapter IV.	(D.) That for a period of more than forty years, that is to say, from 1821 to 1867, the subjects and vessels of Great Britain and the United States and other nations continued in increasing numbers to navigate, trade, and fish in the waters of Behring Sea, and that during the whole of that period no attempt was made on the part of Russia to reassert or claim any dominion or jurisdiction over the non-territorial waters of that sea; but that, on the contrary, the right of all nations to navigate, fish, and exercise common rights therein was fully recognized.

(E.) That at the time of the acquisition of Alaska by the United States pursuant to the Treaty of the 30th March, 1867, Russia had no rights in respect of Behring Sea other than those which belonged to her as possessing territories washed by its waters, and could not transmit to the United States any rights of exclusive dominion or control over navigation and fishing in non-territorial waters, and the United States of America acquiring as they did all the rights of Russia, acquired no more.

Further, that at the time of the acquisition the United States of America was fully alive to the fact that the non-territorial waters of Behring Sea were open to the ships of all nations for the purpose of the exercise of the common rights of navigation and fishing.

That as to the rights which Russia possessed at the time of the Treaty of 1867, and which were transferred to the United States by virtue of that Treaty, the ordinary rule as to the extent of maritime jurisdiction applied.

Admitting, in the consideration of this question, that Russia's title before 1867 to the coast of Behring Sea and to the islands within those waters was complete, an examination of the principles of international law and the practice of nations will show that her jurisdiction (subject to the question of embayed or inland waters) was confined to the distance of 1 marine league or 3 miles from her shores.

Chapter V.

Authorities as to the 3-mile limit.

Ortolan, in his "Diplomatie de la Mer," pp. 145, 153 (édition 1864), says:—

Ortolan.

"On doit ranger sur la même ligne que les rades et les ports, les golfes et les baies et tous les enfoncements connus sous d'autres dénominations, lorsque ces enfoncements, formés par les terres d'un même État, ne dépassent pas en largeur la double portée du canon, ou lorsque l'entrée peut en être gouvernée par l'artillerie, ou qu'elle est défendue naturellement par des îles, par des bancs, ou par des roches. Dans tous ces cas, en effet, il est vrai de dire que ces golfes ou ces baies sont en la puissance de l'État maître du territoire qui les enserre. Cet État en a la possession: tous les raisonnements que nous avons fait à l'égard des rades et des ports peuvent se répéter ici.

Proceedings of Halifax Fisheries Commission, 1877, p. 163.

* * * * *

"Les bords et rivages de la mer qui baigne les côtes d'un État sont les limites maritimes *naturelles* de cet État. Mais pour la protection, pour la défense plus efficace de ces limites naturelles, la coutume générale des nations, d'accord avec beaucoup de Traités publics, permet de tracer sur mer à une distance convenable des côtes, et

Ortolan, p. 153.

suivant leurs contours, une ligne imaginaire qui doit être considérée comme la frontière maritime artificielle. Tout bâtiment qui se trouve à terre de cette ligne est dit être *dans les eaux* de l'État dont elle limite le droit de souveraineté et de juridiction."

Case of the "Washington." Mr. Joshua Bates' decision.

Under the clauses of the Convention of the 8th February, 1853, the case of the "Washington" (which had been seized in the Bay of Fundy and confiscated in the Vice-Admiralty Court at Yarmouth, N.S.) came before the Joint Commission for settlement of claims in London, and on the disagreement of the Commissioners was decided by the Umpire, Mr. Joshua Bates, in favour of the United States. In his decision he said:—

Proceedings of Halifax Fisheries Commission, 1877, p. 152.

"The question turns, so far as relates to the Treaty stipulations, on the meaning given to the word 'bays' in the Treaty of 1783. By that Treaty, the Americans had no right to dry and cure fish on the shores and *bays* of Newfoundland; but they had that right on the shores, *coasts, bays, harbours,* and *creeks* of Nova Scotia; and, as they must land to cure fish on the shores, bays, and creeks, they were evidently admitted to the shores *of the bays, &c.* By the Treaty of 1818 the same right is granted to cure fish on the coasts, bays, &c., of Newfoundland; but the Americans relinquished that right, *and the right to fish within 3 miles* of the coasts, bays, &c., *of Nova Scotia.* Taking it for granted that the framers of the treaty intended that the word 'bay' or 'bays' should have the sa— meaning in all cases, and no mention being made of headlands, there appears no doubt that the 'Washington,' in fishing 10 miles from the shore, violated no stipulations of the Treaty.

"It was urged, on behalf of the British Government, that by 'coasts,' 'bays,' &c., is understood an imaginary line drawn along the coast from headland to headland, and that the jurisdiction of Her Majesty extends 3 marine miles outside of this line; thus closing all the bays on the coast or shore, and that great body of water called the Bay of Fundy, against Americans and others, making the latter a British bay. This doctrine of the headlands is new, and has received a proper limit in the convention between France and Great Britain of the 2nd August, 1839; in which 'it is agreed that the distance of 3 miles, fixed as the general limit for the exclusive right of fishery upon the coasts of the two countries, shall, with respect to bays the mouths of which do not exceed 10 miles in width, be measured from a straight line drawn from headland to headland.'

"The Bay of Fundy is from 65 to 75 miles wide and 130 to 140 miles long; it has several bays on its coast; thus the word 'bay,' as applied to this great body of water, has the same meaning as that applied to the Bay of Biscay, the Bay of Bengal, over which no nation can have the right to assume sovereignty. One of the headlands of the Bay of Fundy is in the United States, and ships bound to Passamaquoddy must sail through a large space of it. The islands of Grand Menan (British) and Little Menan (American) are situated nearly on a line from headland to headland. These islands, as represented in all geographies, are situated in the Atlantic Ocean. The conclusion is, therefore, in my mind irresistible that the Bay of Fundy is not a British bay, nor a bay within the meaning of the word as used in the Treaties of 1783 and 1818."

The Agent for the United States before the Halifax Fisheries Commission, 1877, quotes this decision, and adds the following note :—

"This Convention between France and Great Britain extended the headland doctrine to bays 10 miles wide; thus going beyond the general rule of international law, according to which no bays are treated as within the territorial jurisdiction of a State which are more than 6 miles wide on a straight line measured from one headland to the other." *Proceedings of Halifax Fisheries Commission, 1877, p. 153 (note).*

The principle of the marine league was in 1872 applied by Mr. Boutwell, United States' Secretary to the Treasury, in his letter of instructions to the Collector of Customs at San Francisco, dated 19th April, 1872, already quoted, as follows :— *Secretary Boutwell's opinion. See ante, pp. 108, 109.*

"I do not see that the United States would have the jurisdiction or power to drive off parties going up there for that purpose [to take fur-seals], unless they made such attempt within a marine league of the shore."

The same principle was affirmed in respect of the waters now in question by Mr. Fish, the United States' Secretary of State, who wrote to the United States' Legation in Russia on the 1st December, 1875 :— *Secretary Fish's opinion. See ante, p. 109.*

"There was reason to hope that the practice, which formerly prevailed with powerful nations, of regarding seas and bays, usually of large extent near their coast, as closed to any foreign commerce or fishery not specially licensed by them, was, without exception, a pretension of the past, and that no nation would claim exemption from the general rules of public law which limits its maritime jurisdiction to a marine league from its coast. We should particularly regret if Russia should insist on any such pretension." *Wharton's "Digest," sec. 32, p. 106.*

The same position was taken up by the United States in their brief filed with the Halifax Fisheries Commission in 1877.

The Agent of the United States at Halifax,

after setting out the various authorities under this head concluded as follows:—

<small>Authorities quoted by the United States in Halifax Fisheries Commission.

Proceedings of Halifax Fisheries Commission, 1877, p. 162.</small>

"The jurisdiction of a State or country over its adjoining waters is limited to 3 miles from low-water mark along its sea-coast, and the same rule applies equally to bays and gulfs whose width exceeds 6 miles from headland to headland. Property in and dominion over the sea can only exist as to those portions capable of permanent possession; that is, of a possession from the land, which possession can only be maintained by artillery. At one mile beyond the reach of coast-guns there is no more possession than in mid-ocean. This is the rule laid down by almost all the writers on international law."

As to inland seas and seas over which empire may extend, the following authorities were referred to by the Agent in the same brief:—

<small>Vattel.

Ibid., p. 162.</small>

"At present," says Vattel, "Law of Nations," Book 1, ch. xxiii, §§ 289, 291, "the whole space of the sea within cannon-shot of the coast is considered as making a part of the territory; and, for that reason, a vessel taken under the guns of a neutral fortress is not a good prize.

"All we have said of the parts of the sea near the coast may be said more particularly, and with much greater reason, of the roads, bays, and straits, as still more capable of being occupied, and of greater importance to the safety of the country. But I speak of the bays and straits of small extent, and not of those great parts of the sea to which these names are sometimes given—as Hudson's Bay and the Straits of Magellan—over which the Empire cannot extend, and still less a right of property. A bay whose entrance may be defended may be possessed and rendered subject to the laws of the Sovereign; and it is of importance that it should be so, since the country may be much more easily insulted in such a place than on the coast, open to the winds and the impetuosity of the waves."

<small>Bluntschli.

Ibid., p. 163.</small>

Professor Bluntschli, in his "Law of Nations," Book 4, §§ 302, 309, states the rule in the same way:—

"When the frontier of a State is formed by the open sea, the part of the sea over which the State can from the shore make its power respected—*i.e.*, a portion of the sea extending as far as a cannon-shot from the coast—is considered as belonging to the territory of that State. Treaties or agreements can establish other and more precise limits."

"*Note.*—The extent practised of this sovereignty has remarkably increased since the invention of far-shooting cannon. This is the consequence of the improvements made in the means of defence, of which the State makes use. The sovereignty of States over the sea extended originally only to a stone's-throw from the coast; later, to an arrow-shot; fire-arms were invented, and by rapid progress we have arrived to the far-shooting cannon of the present age. But still we preserve the principle : ' *Terræ dominium finitur, ubi finitur armorum vis.*' "

"Within certain limits, there are submitted to the sovereignty of the bordering State :—

"(*a*.) The portion of the sea placed within a cannon-shot of the shore.

"(*b*.) Harbours.

"(*c*.) Gulfs.

"(*d*.) Roadsteads."

"*Note.*—Certain portions of the sea are so nearly joined to the *terra firma*, that, in some measure at least, they ought to form a part of the territory of the bordering State; they are considered as accessories to the *terra firma*. The safety of the State, and the public quiet, are so dependent on them that they cannot be contended, in certain gulfs, with the portion of the sea lying under the fire of cannon from the coast. These exceptions from the general rule of the liberty of the sea can only be made for weighty reasons, and when the extent of the arm of the sea is not large; thus, Hudson's Bay and the Gulf of Mexico evidently are a part of the open sea. No one disputes the power of England over the arm of the sea lying between the Isle of Wight and the English coast, which could not be admitted for the sea lying between England and Ireland; the English Admiralty has, however, sometimes maintained the theory of 'narrow seas;' and has tried, but without success, to keep for its own interest, under the name of 'King's Chambers,' some considerable extents of the sea."

Klüber, "Droit des Gens Modernes de l'Europe (Paris, édition 1831)," tom. i, p. 216 :—   Kluber.

"Au territoire maritime d'un État appartiennent les   Proceedings of
districts maritimes, ou parages susceptibles d'une pos-   Halifax Fisheries
session exclusive, sur lesquels l'État a acquis (par occu-   Commission, 1877,
pation ou convention) et continué la souveraineté. Sont   p. 163.
de ce nombre (1) les parties de l'océan qui avoisinent le
territoire continental de l'État, du moins, d'après l'opinion
presque généralement adoptée, autant qu'elles se trouvent
sous la portée du canon qui serait placé sur le rivage ;
(2) les parties de l'océan qui s'étendent dans le territoire
continental de l'État, si elles peuvent être gouvernées par le
canon des deux bords, ou que l'entrée seulement on peut
être défendue aux vaisseaux (golfes, baies, et calos) ;
(3) les détroits qui séparent deux continents, et qui également sont sous la portée du canon placé sur le rivage, ou
dont l'entrée et la sortie peuvent être défendues (détroit,
canal, bosphore, sonde). Sont encore du même nombre :
(4) les golfes, détroits, et mers avoisinant le territoire
continental d'un État, lesquels, quoiqu'ils ne soient pas
entièrement sous la portée du canon, sont néanmoins
reconnus par d'autres Puissances comme mer fermée,

c'est-à-dire, comme soumis à une domination, et, par conséquent, inaccessibles aux vaisseaux étrangers qui n'ont point obtenu la permission d'y naviguer."

This view, moreover, was emphatically maintained on behalf of the United States on the occasion of the seizures in the year 1887.

The following is the extract from the Brief of the United States on this occasion :—

Brief for the United States, Sitka, in 1887.

Brief for the United States Filed at Sitka October 12, 1887, "New York Herald," October 18, 1887. Blue Book, "United States No. 2 (1890)," p. 112. See Appendix, vol. iii.

"Concerning the doctrine of international law establishing what is known as the marine league belt, which extends the jurisdiction of a nation into adjacent seas for the distance of 1 marine league, or 3 miles from its shores, and following all the indentations and sinuosities of its coast, there is at this day no room for discussion. It must be accepted as the settled law of nations. It is sustained by the highest authorities, law-writers, and jurists. It has been sanctioned by the United States since the foundation of the Government. It was affirmed by Mr. Jefferson, Secretary of State, as early as 1793, and has been reaffirmed by his successors—Mr. Pickering, in 1796; Mr. Madison, in 1807; Mr. Webster, in 1842; Mr. Buchanan, in 1849; Mr. Seward, in 1862, 1863, and 1864; Mr. Fish,* in 1875; Mr. Evarts, in 1879 and 1881; and Mr. Bayard, in 1886." (Wheaton's [Wharton] "International Law," vol. i, sec. 32, pp. 100 and 109.)

See Lord Lansdowne to Mr. Stanhope. November 27, 1896. Blue Book, "United States No. 2 (1890)," p. 28. Appendix, vol. iii.

"Sanctioned thus by an unbroken line of precedents covering the first century of our national existence, the United States would not abandon this doctrine if they could; they could not if they would."

---

* This probably refers to Mr. Fish's letter already quoted at p. 109, or to his letter to Sir E. Thornton, dated the 22nd January, 1875, which is as follows:—

"The instruction from the Foreign Office to Mr. Watson of the 25th December last, a copy of which was communicated by that gentleman to this Department in his note of the 17th October, directs him to ascertain the views of this Government in regard to the extent of maritime jurisdiction which can properly be claimed by any Power, and whether we have ever recognized the claim of Spain to a 6-mile limit, or have ever protested against such claim.

"In reply, I have the honour to inform you that this Government has uniformly, under every Administration which has had occasion to consider the subject, objected to the pretension of Spain adverted to, upon the same ground and in similar terms to those contained in the instruction of the Earl of Derby.

"We have understood and asserted that, pursuant to public law, no nation can rightfully claim jurisdiction at sea beyond a marine league from the coast.

"This opinion on our part has sometimes been said to be inconsistent with the facts that, by the law of the United States, revenue cutters are authorized to board vessels anywhere within 4 leagues of their coasts, and that by the Treaty of Guadalupe-Hidalgo, so called between the United States and Mexico, of the 2nd February, 1848, the boundary-line between the dominions of the parties begins in the Gulf of Mexico, 3 leagues from land."

And he proceeds to explain these two instances as being exceptional. . . . (Wharton, "International Law," vol. l, p. 108.)

The Russian claim to extraordinary jurisdiction was expressly founded on a supposed right to hold a portion of the Pacific as *mare clausum*, because that nation claimed the territory on both sides. Even if this claim had been well founded the Treaty of 1867 destroyed it, since the sea was no longer shut in or surrounded by the territory of one nation.

Effect of cession of Alaska on mare clausum doctrine.

On this subject Ortolan writes:—

Ortolan.

"'Quant aux mers particulières et intérieures, un droit exclusif de domaine et de souveraineté de la part d'une nation sur une telle mer n'est incontestable qu'autant que cette mer est totalement enclavée dans le territoire de telle sorte qu'elle en fait partie intégrante, et qu'elle ne peut absolument servir de lien de communication et de commerce qu'entre les seuls citoyens de cette nation. Alors, en effet, aucune des causes qui font obstacle soit à la propriété, soit à l'empire des mers, ne trouve ici son application. Mais du moment que plusieurs États différents possèdent des côtes autour de cette mer, aucun d'eux ne peut s'en dire propriétaire ni souverain à l'exclusion des autres.'"

Ortolan, "Règles Internationales et Diplomatie de la Mer," 4e édition, tom. i, p. 147.

Sir Travers Twiss writes to the same effect:—

Twiss.

"If a sea is *entirely inclosed* by the territory of a nation, and has no other communication with the ocean than by a channel, of which that nation may take possession, it appears that such a sea is no less capable of being occupied and becoming property than the land, and it ought to follow the fate of the country that surrounds it."

"Rights and Duties of Nations in time of Peace," 1884, p. 293.

So Halleck says:—

Halleck.

"21. It is generally admitted that the territory of a State includes the seas, lakes, and rivers entirely inclosed within its limits. Thus, so long as the shores of the Black Sea were exclusively possessed by Turkey, that sea might, with propriety, be considered as a *mare clausum*; and there seemed no reason to question the right of the Ottoman Porte to exclude other nations from navigating the passage which connects it with the Mediterranean, both shores of this passage being also portions of the Turkish territory. But when Turkey lost a part of her possessions bordering upon this sea, and Russia had formed her commercial establishments on the shores of the Euxine, both that Empire and other Maritime Powers became entitled to participate in the commerce of the Black Sea, and consequently to the free navigation of the Dardanelles and the Bosphorus. This right was expressly recognized by the Treaty of Adrianople in 1829.

Halleck's International Law, vol. i, cap. 6, pp. 143–145.

"22. The great inland lakes and their navigable outlets, are considered as subject to the same rule as inland seas: where inclosed within the limits of a single State, they are regarded as belonging to the territory of that State; but if different nations occupy their borders, the rule of *mare clausum* cannot be applied to the navigation and use of their waters."

The view expressed by the above authorities has been officially adopted by an accredited Representative of the United States, so that it is perhaps unnecessary to insist further upon it in this connection.

Mr. Hoffman.

On the 11th March, 1882, Mr. Hoffman wrote from the Legation of the United States at St. Petersburg to Mr. Frelinghuysen, Secretary of State, in a letter already quoted:—

Mr. Hoffman to Mr. Frelinghuysen, March 14, 1882. 50th Congress, 2nd Sess., Senate Ex. Doc. No. 106, p. 260. See Appendix, vol. ii, Part II, No. 13.

"In the time when Russia owned the whole of these islands her Representatives in Siberia claimed that the Sea of Okhotsk was a *mare clausum*, for that Russian jurisdiction extended from island to island and over 2 marine leagues of intermediate sea from Japan to Kamtchatka.

"But about five years ago Russia ceded the southern group of those islands to Japan in return for the half of the Island of Saghalien, which belonged to that Power.

"As soon as this was done, it became impossible for the Siberian authorities to maintain their claim. My informant was not aware that this claim had ever been seriously made at St. Petersburg."

And on the 27th March, 1882, he further wrote:—

Mr. Hoffman to Mr. Frelinghuysen, March 27, 1882. 50th Congress, 2nd Sess., Senate Ex. Doc. No. 106, p. 261. See Appendix, vol. ii, Part II, No. 14.

"I do not think that Russia claims that the Sea of Okhotsk is a *mare clausum*, over which she has exclusive jurisdiction. If she does, her claim is not a tenable one, since the cession of part of the group of the Kurile Islands to Japan, if it ever were tenable at any time."

Professor Angell.

See Appendix, vol. i, No. 8.

Professor James B. Angell, one of the United States' Plenipotentiaries in the negotiation of the Fisheries Treaty at Washington in 1888, and an eminent jurist, in an article entitled "American Rights in Behring Sea," in "The Forum" for November 1889, wrote:—

"Can we sustain a claim that Behring Sea is a closed sea, and so subject to our control? It is, perhaps, impossible to frame a definition of a closed sea which the publicists of all nations will accept. Vattel's closed sea is one 'entirely inclosed by the land of a nation, with only a communication with the ocean by a channel of which that nation may take possession.' Hautefeuille substantially adopts this statement, asserting more specifically, however, that the channel must be narrow enough to be defended from the shores. Perels, one of the more eminent of the later German writers, practically accepts Hautefeuille's definition. But so narrow a channel or opening as that indicated by the eminent French writer can hardly be insisted on. Probably, most authorities will regard it as a reasonable requirement that the entrance to the sea should be narrow enough to make the naval occupation of it easy or practicable. We, at least, may be expected to prescribe no definition which would make the Gulf of St. Lawrence a closed sea.

"Behring Sea is not inclosed wholly by our territory. From the most western island in our possession to the nearest point on the Asiatic shore is more than 300 miles. From our most western island (Attou) to the nearest Russian island (Copper Island) is 183 miles. The sea from east to west measures about 1,100 miles, and from north to south fully 800 miles. The area of the sea must be at least two-thirds as great as that of the Mediterranean, and more than twice that of the North Sea. The Straits of Gibraltar are less than 9 miles wide. The chief entrance to the Gulf of St. Lawrence, which is entirely surrounded by British territory, is only about 50 miles in width. Behring Sea is open on the north by the straits, 36 miles wide, which form a passage way to the Arctic Ocean. On what grounds and after what modern precedent we could set up a claim to hold this great sea, with its wide approaches, as a *mare clausum*, it is not easy to see."

Dana, in a note to Wheaton's "Elements," says :—   Mr. Dana.

"The only question now is, whether a given sea or sound is, in fact, as a matter of politico-physical geography, within the exclusive jurisdiction of one nation. The claim of several nations, whose borders surround a large open sea, to combine and make it *mare clausum* against the rest of the world, cannot be admitted. The making of such a claim to the Baltic was the infirmity of the position taken up by the Armed Neutrality in 1780 and 1800, and in the Russian Declaration of War against England in 1807."   Wheaton, 8th edition, by Mr. Dana, 1866, section 187 (note).

It is further claimed, on behalf of Great Britain—

(F.) That from the acquisition of Alaska by the United States in 1867 down to the year 1886 no attempt was made by the United States to limit or interfere with the right of the subjects of Great Britain or of any other nation to navigate and fish in the non-territorial waters of Behring Sea.   Chapter VI.

(G.) That the original ground upon which the vessels seized in 1886 and 1887 were condemned rested upon a claim to treat Behring Sea as *mare clausum*, and as having been conveyed as such, in part, by Russia to the United States.   Chapter VII.

That the contention of the United States has subsequently been rested upon a claim to exclusive jurisdiction over a space of 100 miles from the coast of the United States' territory.

That subsequently a further claim has been raised to an alleged special right of protection of or property in the fur-seal.

As to Point 5 of Article VI—

General conclusions.

Chapter VIII.
Alleged right of protection.

That, as regards the right claimed by the United States of protection of or property in fur-seals when found outside the ordinary 3-mile limit, no property exists, or is known to international law in animals *feræ naturæ* until reduced into possession by capture, and no nation has any right to claim property in such animals when found outside territorial waters. The only right is to prevent the ships and subjects of other nations from entering territorial waters for the purpose of capturing such animals.

Analogous questions.

Upon analogous questions similar principles have been generally maintained and recognized.

Right of search on high seas.

Thus, with reference to the right to search neutral vessels upon the high seas—In 1804, during the war with France, Great Britain claimed to search neutral vessels on the high seas, and to seize her own subjects when found serving under a neutral flag.

Mr. Madison to Mr. Monroe, January 5, 1804. American State Papers, Foreign Relations, vol. ii, p. 730.

The position taken on this subject by the United States was not only in opposition to such a right, but that country insisted that *in no case* did the sovereignty of any nation extend beyond its own dominions and its own vessels on the high seas.

Slave Trade.

A similar view has been adopted by all nations in relation to the Slave Trade.

Although it cannot properly be argued that the taking of seals in any manner whatever is comparable with the immorality or injustice attaching to the Slave Trade, yet, even in the case of vessels engaged in that trade, the rights of nations have not been allowed to be overruled on such pleas.

Upon this point legal authorities both in the United States and in Great Britain are quite clear.

Case of "Le Louis" engaged in Slave Trade and seized.

In 1816 a French vessel ("Le Louis") sailing from Martinique, destined on a voyage to the coast of Africa and back, was captured 10 or 12 leagues to the southward of Cape Mesurada, by the "Queen Charlotte" cutter, and carried to Sierra Leone. She was proceeded against in the Vice-Admiralty Court of that colony.

"Le Louis," 1816. See Dodson's Admiralty Cases, vol. ii, p. 210.

It was alleged that the vessel was fitted out for the purpose of carrying on the African Slave Trade, after that trade had been abolished by the internal laws of France, and by the Treaty between Great Britain and France.

Slave Trade.

Case of "Le Louis."

The King's Advocate admitted the proposition to be true *generally* that the right of visitation and search does not exist in time of peace, but denied it to be so *universally*. Occasions, he argued, may and must arise, at a period when no hostilities exist, in which an exercise of this power would be justifiable. The rule of law could not be maintained as a universal proposition, but was subject to exceptions, and within those exceptions must be included the present transaction, which was a transgression, not only of municipal law, but likewise of the general law of nations. In whatever light the Slave Trade might have been viewed in former times, it must no longer be deemed within the protection of the law of nations. Since the Declaration of the Congress of Vienna, that the Slave Trade was repugnant to the principles of humanity and of universal morality, traffic in slaves must be considered a crime, and it was the right and duty of every nation to prevent the commission of crime. On the whole, he submitted that the "Le Louis," having been engaged in a traffic prohibited by the laws of her own country, and contrary to the general laws of humanity and justice, ought not to be restored to the claimant.

Lord Stowell's Judgment. Seizure not justified.

Sir William Scott, afterwards Lord Stowell, in the British High Court of Admiralty, held, however, that trading in slaves was not a crime by universal law of nations. He observed :—

" Neither this Court nor any other can carry its private apprehensions, independent of law, into its public judgments on the quality of actions. It must conform to the judgment of the law upon that subject ; and acting as a Court in the administration of law, it cannot attribute criminality to an act where the law imputes none. It must look to the legal standard of morality ; and upon a question of this nature, that standard must be found in the law of nations as fixed and evidenced by general and ancient and admitted practice, by Treaties and by the general tenour of the laws and ordinances and the formal transactions of civilized States. *See Dodson's Admiralty Cases, vol. II, p. 249.*

" . . . . Much stress is laid upon a solemn declaration of very eminent persons assembled in Congress, whose rank, high as it is, is by no means the most respectable foundation of the weight of their opinion that this traffic is contrary to all religion and morality. Great as the reverence due to such authorities may be, they cannot I think be admitted to have the force of overruling the established course of the general law of nations." *Ibid., p. 252*

*　　*　　*　　*　　*

Slave Trade.

Case of "La Louis."
See Dodson's Admiralty Cases, vol. II, p. 252.

Ibid., p. 256.

"It is next said that every country has a right to enforce its own navigation laws; and so it certainly has, so far as it does not interfere with the rights of others. But it has no right, in consequence, to visit and search all the apparent vessels of other countries on the high seas."

* * * *

"It is said, and with just concern, that if not permitted in time of peace, it will be extremely difficult to suppress the Traffic. It will be so, and no man can deny that the suppression, however desirable, and however sought, is attended with enormous difficulties; difficulties which have baffled the most zealous endeavours for many years. To every man it must have been evident that without a general and sincere concurrence of all the Maritime States, in the principle and in the proper modes of pursuing it, comparatively but little of positive good could be acquired; so far at least as the interests of the victims of this commerce were concerned in it; and to every man who looks to the rival claims of these States, to their established habits of trade, to their real or pretended wants, to their different modes of thinking, and to their real mode of acting upon this particular subject, it must be equally evident that such a concurrence was matter of very difficult attainment. But the difficulty of the attainment will not legalize measures that are otherwise illegal. To press forward to a great principle by breaking through every other great principle that stands in the way of its establishment; to force the way to the liberation of Africa by trampling on the independence of other States in Europe; in short, to procure an eminent good by means that are unlawful; is as little consonant to private morality as to public justice. Obtain the concurrence of other nations, if you can, by application, by remonstrance, by example, by every peaceable instrument which man can employ to attract the consent of man. But a nation is not justified in assuming rights that do not belong to her, merely because she means to apply them to a laudable purpose; nor in setting out upon a moral crusade of converting other nations by acts of unlawful force. Nor is it to be argued that because other nations approve the ultimate purpose, they must therefore submit to every measure which any one State or its subjects may inconsiderately adopt for its attainment."

In accordance with this view of the law the Judgment of the Vice-Admiralty Cour. of Sierra Leone, condemning the French ship for being employed in the Slave Trade and for forcibly resisting the search of the King of England's cruizers, was reversed.

Case of the "Antelope." United States' Supreme Court to same effect.

Wheaton, Report, vol. x, p. 66.

The decision of the Supreme Court of the United States in the case of the "Antelope" is to the same effect. There Chief Justice Marshall delivered the opinion of the Court, holding that the Slave Trade, though contrary to the law of nature, was not in conflict with the law of nations:—

"No principle of general law is more universally acknowledged than the perfect equality of nations. Russia and Geneva have equal rights. It results from this equality, that no one can rightfully impose a rule on another. Each legislates for itself, but its legislation can operate on itself alone. A right, then, which is vested in all by the consent of all, can be devested only by consent; and this trade, in which all have participated, must remain lawful to those who cannot be induced to relinquish it. As no nation can prescribe a rule for others, none can make a law of nations; and this traffic remains lawful to those whose Governments have not forbidden it.

"If it is consistent with the law of nations, it cannot in itself be piracy. It can be made so only by statute; and the obligation of the statute cannot transcend the legislative power of the State which may enact it.

"If it be neither repugnant to the law of nations, nor piracy, it is almost superfluous to say in this Court that the right of bringing in for adjudication in time of peace, even where the vessel belongs to a nation which has prohibited the trade, cannot exist. The Courts of no country execute the penal laws of another, and the course of the American Government on the subject of visitation and search, would decide any case in which that right had been exercised by an American cruizer on the vessel of a foreign nation not violating our municipal laws, against the captors.

"It follows, that a foreign vessel engaged in the African slave trade, captured on the high seas in time of peace, by an American cruizer, and brought in for adjudication, would be restored."

The subject is fully discussed in Mr. Dana's note No. 108 to Wheaton's International Law (p. 258), where it is said of Chief Justice Marshall, in Church *versus* Hubbart, 2 Cranch, 187 :—

"It is true that Chief Justice Marshall admitted the right of a nation to secure itself against intended violations of its laws, by seizures made within reasonable limits, as to which, he said, nations must exercise comity and concession, and the exact extent of which was not settled; and, in the case before the Court, the 4 leagues were not treated as rendering the seizure illegal. This remark must now be treated as an unwarranted admission. . . . It may be said that the principle is settled that municipal seizures cannot be made, for any purpose, beyond territorial waters. It is also settled that the limit of these waters is, in the absence of treaty, the marine league or the cannon-shot. It cannot now be successfully maintained, either that municipal visits and search may be made beyond the territorial waters for special purposes, or that there are different bounds of that territory for different objects. But, as the line of territorial waters, if not fixed, is dependent on the unsettled range of artillery fire, and, if fixed, must be by an arbitrary measure, the courts, in the earlier cases, were not strict as to standards of distance,

---

Slave Trade.

Case of the "Antelope."

Wheaton, Report, vol. x, p. 122.

Mr. Dana.

Wheaton, "International Law," 8th edition, by Mr. Dana, 1866, p. 359.

Ibid., p. 260.

where no foreign Powers intervened in the causes. In later times, it is safe to infer that judicial as well as political tribunals will insist on one line of marine territorial jurisdiction for the exercise of force on foreign vessels, in time of peace, for all purposes alike."

It is an axiom of international maritime law that such action is only admissible in the case of piracy or in pursuance of special international agreement. This principle has been universally admitted by jurists, and was very distinctly laid down by President Tyler in his Special Message to Congress, dated the 27th February, 1843, when, after acknowledging the right to detain and search a vessel on suspicion of piracy, he goes on to say:—

President Tyler.

State Papers, by Hertslet, vol. xxxii, p. 575.

"With this single exception, no nation has, in time of peace, any authority to detain the ships of another upon the high seas, on any pretext whatever, outside the territorial jurisdiction."

Article VII.

Article VII.

Consideration of Regulations postponed.

Great Britain maintains, in the light of the facts and arguments which have been adduced on the points included in the VIth Article of the Treaty, that her concurrence is necessary to the establishment of any Regulations which limit or control the rights of British subjects to exercise their right of the pursuit and capture of seals in the non-territorial waters of Behring Sea. The further consideration of any proposed Regulations, and of the evidence proper to be considered by the Tribunal in connection therewith, must of necessity be for the present postponed.

Chapter X.

Recapitulation of Argument.

The following are the propositions of law and fact, which, it is maintained on behalf of Great Britain, have been established in the foregoing Case:—

1. The sea now known as Behring Sea is an open sea, free to the vessels of all nations, and the right of all nations to navigate and fish in the waters of Behring Sea, other than the territorial waters thereof, is a natural right.

2. No assertion of jurisdiction by Russia, the United States, or any other nation could limit or restrict the right of all nations to the free use of the open sea for navigation or fishing.

3. At no time prior to the Treaty of the 30th March, 1867, did Russia possess any exclusive jurisdiction in the non-territorial waters of the sea now known as Behring Sea.

4. At no time prior to the said cession did Russia assert or exercise any exclusive rights in the seal fisheries in the non-territorial waters of the sea now known as Behring Sea.

5. The attempt by Russia in the year 1821 to restrict the freedom of navigation and fishing by the subjects of other nations than Russia in the non-territorial waters of Behring Sea was immediately and effectually resisted by Great Britain and the United States of America.

6. The claims of Russia to limit and interfere with the rights of navigation and fishing by other nations in the waters of Behring Sea, other than the territorial waters thereof, were never recognized or conceded by Great Britain.

7. The protests raised and the objections taken by Great Britain to the claims of Russia to limit such free right of navigation and fishing were acquiesced in by Russia; and no attempt was ever made by Russia to again assert

Recapitulation of Argument.

or enforce any such supposed right to exclude or limit the rights of other nations to navigate or fish in the waters of the sea now known as Behring Sea, other than the territorial waters thereof.

8. The assertion of rights by Russia in the year 1821, and her ineffectual attempt to limit the rights of navigation and fishing, was inoperative and had no effect upon the rights of other nations.

9. The body of water now known as the Behring Sea was included in the phrase "Pacific Ocean," as used in the Treaty of 1825 between Great Britain and Russia.

10. From the year 1821 down to 1886 the vessels of Great Britain have continuously, and without interruption or interference, exercised the rights of navigation and fishing in the waters of Behring Sea other than the territorial waters thereof.

11. The right of all nations to navigate and fish in the waters of Behring Sea, other than the territorial waters thereof, have been repeatedly recognized and admitted both by Russia and by the United States of America.

12. Whatever territorial rights passed to the United States under and by virtue of the Treaty of the 30th March, 1867, Russia had not the right to transmit, and the United States did not acquire, any jurisdiction over or rights in the seal fisheries in any part of the sea now known as Behring Sea, other than in the territorial waters thereof.

13. The Treaty of Cession of the 30th March, 1867, did not convey anything more than ordinary territorial dominion.

14. From the acquisition of Alaska by the United States in 1867 down to the year 1886, no attempt was made by the United States to assert or exercise any right to limit or interfere with the right of Great Britain, or of any other nation, to navigate and fish in the waters of Behring Sea other than the territorial waters thereof.

Recapitulation of Argument.

15. The sole right of the United States in respect of the protection of seals is that incident to territorial possession, including the right to prevent the subjects of other nations from entering upon land belonging to the United States, or the territorial waters thereof, so as to prevent their capturing seals or any other animals or fish either on such lands or in such territorial waters.

16. The United States have not, nor has any subject of the United States, any property in fur-seals until they have been reduced into possession by capture, and the property so acquired endures so long only as they are retained in control.

17. Fur-seals are animals *feræ naturæ*, and the United States has no right of protection or property in fur-seals when found outside the ordinary 3-mile limit, whether such seals frequent the islands of the United States in Behring Sea or not.

18. The right of the subjects of all nations to navigate and fish in the non-territorial waters of the sea now known as Behring Sea remains and exists free and unfettered, and cannot be limited or interfered with except with the concurrence of any nations affected.

19. No regulations affecting British subjects can be established for the protection and preservation of the fur-seal in the non-territorial waters of Behring Sea without the concurrence of Great Britain.

CONCLUSION.

Conclusion.

It is submitted on behalf of Great Britain to the Tribunal of Arbitration, that the questions raised in this Arbitration are of far greater importance than the mere preservation of a particular industry; they involve the right of every nation of the world to navigate on and fish in the high seas, and to exercise without interference the common rights of the human race; they involve the question of the right of one nation by Proclamation to limit and interfere with rights which are the common heritage of all mankind. In defence of these rights and in the interests of all civilized nations, the above arguments are respectfully urged upon the consideration of the Tribunal.

Schedule of Claims.

The SCHEDULE annexed to this Case contains particulars in connection with the claims presented under Article VIII of the Treaty of Arbitration, and the facts and evidence contained in the Schedule are submitted to the consideration of the Tribunal for the purposes stated at p. 12 of this Case.

www.ingramcontent.com/pod-product-compliance
Lightning Source LLC
Chambersburg PA
CBHW022117160426
43197CB00009B/1069